Moving Forward

A Woman's Guide to Healing and Moving on After a Breakup

by Carli Lance

Lance, Carli 1977 -

ISBN 978-1-7777998-0-9 (Paperback)
ISBN 978-1-7777998-1-6 (eBook)

Edited by Christine Bode
Book production by Dawn James, Publish and Promote
Cover, layout and interior design by Publish and Promote.

Illustrations designed by Freepik

Printed and bound in Canada.

Note to the reader: The events in this book are based on the writers' memories from her perspective. Certain names have been changed to protect the identity of those mentioned. Any similarity to real persons, places, incidents, or actions is coincidental. The information is provided for educational purposes only. In the event you use any of the information in this book for yourself, which is your constitutional right, the author and publisher assume no responsibility for your actions.

Contents

Preface

Can we have it all?

That's the question we are often asked as women. What does that even mean? Does anybody truly have it all? I contend that this is entirely the wrong question. Maybe we should be asking ourselves how we use what we are given so that we can keep moving forward. Some people are blessed with a great career but challenged with their health. Others are challenged in the athletic department but blessed by a carefree sense of adventure.

I have so many blessings in my life, it's unreal. I have great kids, I have had career successes, a great group of friends, accessible resources to help me when needed, and a great home but I have been challenged in my relationships to the not-so-fairer sex. As a result, I've become an expert on breakups. I faced the challenges, in this area, presented in my life, squeezed the lessons learned for all they were worth, and have condensed my lessons into this book. How's that for making lemonade? All those breakups (with the occasional makeup) have led me here to you today, to do what I was meant to do: help people. I may have been served my fair share of life's crap sandwiches on a silver platter, but I learned that it's what you decide to do with the crap sandwiches that really matters. And the real trick is figuring out how to manage this challenge and move on.

In early 2007, I was once again experiencing the pain of a breakup. My heart was broken again during another failed relationship. The relationship was short and intense. We both dove in quickly and spent a lot of time together. He was fun, we had fun, and it was fun. However, it fizzled as fast as it started. He wanted "more", and I wanted "more" as well. He had his life, and it was small and consistent. I had a world that I loved and enjoyed it growing bigger and bigger and he wanted nothing to do with that. We broke up on the first day of spring that year and I cried for about ten minutes. I hate breakups. They just suck. I also have come to know that they happen. Whether it is a divorce, a breakup with an intimate partner, or a friendship—it happens.

After that breakup, I found myself single again—not sure what to do with it—but knew I was there again. This time around, I decided to write about how I got through what had become a series of breakups. I mention one above but there were enough of them to give me the right the write this book. I had once been dumped the day before Valentine's Day by a "nice guy." I was betrayed by friends and men—you can put two and two together. I dated one guy that was the epitome of charming, wining and dining, not just me, but my friends as well. He was successful, good-looking, smart—"the package." He turned out to be a raging druggie with serious issues so that ended abruptly, too.

By this point in 2007, I had stories of breakups and I knew I had the ability to move through them.

I completed the first draft of that book, *The Power of Next: A Guide to Getting Through Breakups*, on October 25, 2007. Heartbreak was something I was getting relatively resilient with navigating through, and I knew I had wisdom that might help others. The word "next" was my mantra—it helped me realign my thoughts, focus, goals, and life. I used writing to work through any of my relationship upsets, including friendships. When I faced sleepless nights or was consumed with anger, I would say to myself, "next." It got me into a positive mind frame and helped me believe, hope, and visualize that another opportunity to find bliss was on the horizon.

While I remember writing the book during this time, I barely remember the motivation. Writing a book is not an easy task, so I'm not sure where I found the energy to write it. Shortly after completing the first draft, I cautiously explored a new beau, which led to a relationship after two months. This one also moved quickly, but it was with someone I had known for over nine years. To my surprise, this relationship led to an engagement in April 2008 (yes, ten months later). I printed the first draft of my manuscript, put it in a folder, and let it collect dust in a cabinet. I also married this person.

Fast forward to August 2019. I was sitting on the couch healing from my recent separation. After a wedding, a house, two kids, and many travels later, our marriage ended on June 1, 2019. The now-ex had moved out and we implemented 50/50 custody.

 7

On this August day, the kids were at his house. I was starting to learn how to adapt to having days away from my kids (a personal hell, to which I have yet to get used to) and healing from this sudden divorce. I was searching—searching for tools to navigate the pain, anger, sadness, shame, loneliness, grief, and the many other feelings and challenges divorce brings. I was sifting through paperwork in my cabinet when I stumbled upon, "The Power of Next," the original version of this book. I took it downstairs to my living room, made some coffee, and started reading the "manual" I wrote years before hoping to find tips on how to heal. As I started reading this very rough draft, I found myself beginning to revise the book. Within moments, I found myself committing to writing this book with the new divorce experience in mind.

About a week later, I had already started rewriting the book and I reconnected with a friend who is the current president of a writing group I once belonged to. I told her about my divorce and that I was writing again. I explained the backstory of the book and my goal. She said, "Let's get this done, it's time." Ironically, just a few days before, one of my BFFs in Toronto had said the same thing to me, "It's your time." (No doubt influenced by her recent viewing of *Black Panther*.) My time was clearly becoming a theme. No more excuses. I added the journey of writing this book again to my healing process.

Timing is an interesting thing. As many celebrities have said in award acceptance speeches over the years, there is one place where all the people with the greatest potential are gathered—one place—and that is the graveyard. I felt like I was on track to be one of those people. Not that I am dying per se, but I was getting nothing done and life does what it does well—

 8

keeps moving forward. I wanted more. I wanted to achieve my number one goal which was to write a book (hopefully a best-selling book). I have dabbled in writing for years. I have yet to complete a project and the excuses pile up, including:

- Giving birth
- Raising kids
- Being a wife
- Working full-time
- Being exhausted
- Kids' extracurriculars
- Wanting to focus on my Masters (still incomplete as of this writing)
- Tackling a new job transition
- Travel
- Planning a baby shower
- Planning a bridal shower
- Imposter syndrome
- Collect more than 1,000 brand-new socks for the less fortunate
- Etc.

I also was fiercely protective of what I had. I had a family, a complete, traditional nuclear family: two parents (my ex-husband and I) and two kids. I had a home, one in which I had never lived anywhere longer. I had consistent income in my hard-working career. I was able to volunteer. I was able to call people over for a BBQ and cover the bill. I was able to do more and enjoy more than in my wildest dreams. But it all triggered my anxiety regularly. I was so scared it would all disappear. I was scared that if I wrote a book and was super successful, I would lose it all. I was scared that if I wrote a book and was not successful, I would lose it all. I lived in insane fear. Until one of my fears finally came to the surface: a divorce. The reality was out of my control. I feared something I had no control of, and it happened. However, it shook me up. It made me realize I don't have control over anything. That in turn, made me realize I can still go after this dream. Divorce sucks, breakups suck, failure sucks, but the silver lining is that I'm finishing this book and doing what I've been called to do—to help others.

If you are reading this book, more than likely, you are looking to work through the challenges that a breakup brings to the surface: the emotional, mental, and physical challenges. This book is a toolkit on how to manage and navigate through challenging times. Change is inevitable; therefore, challenging times are inevitable. My goal with these words is to get you off the couch if you have become too comfortable there. Even more so, to help you avoid getting on the couch in the first place. But primarily, I want you to interact and integrate into the world that keeps moving around you as fast as possible. It doesn't take away the pain, no. But it will help you navigate it faster. It will help you be more motivated to stand up. It will let you see, with the abundance of people around you, that all have some sort of tragedy or trauma you may or may not be aware of, and that most are living, laughing, and loving. It will give you hope that you, too, will be here one day—sooner than later is the plan. My goal for this book is for you to transition through this challenge faster, to grow through this, to be better, stronger, smarter, and faster.

The stories I write about here will be brief and bold. I am going to let you into my life and hopefully convince you that I am qualified to write this book. You will hear a lot of cursing and a few spiritual references too because a big part of who I am is a lover of Jesus. Everybody has their tools. Jesus is one of my tools and swearing is another. It might be challenging at times to read this book; it might be uplifting at other points. I hope it is a healthy combination of both. As we travel on this journey, I aim to offer you inner peace, the motivation to love again, and the foresight to see what can happen if you plan the proper steps to get you through the unfortunate, challenging, or traumatizing events in your life. Are you ready? What a silly question—of course, you are! I am here to hold your hand and be your support sister as we journey through this process together.

Maybe we can't have it all, but we can face whatever we are facing, move through it, and move forward. I'm sharing my lessons with you to help you through that journey so that you can start the healing process and move on to whatever you were put on this earth to do. And let me tell you, as I put this book into the world, I have moved on as well. I don't know that the breakups are behind me, but I now have the tools to face them, and my mastery is now focused on living my best, incredible life. And I wish the same for you.

Section 1:

Breakups

"Don't let your past dictate who you are, but let it be a lesson that strengthens the person you'll become."

~ Unknown

Let's Begin With the End

It could not have been a more beautiful day—springtime in the mountains. The mix of fresh blooms and a mountain creek filled the air like a perfect outdoor blend of fresh potpourri. I often take the kids on weekend road trips to Kananaskis or Canmore, Alberta as we like to go on adventures, even small, quick ones. I am a quality time person—all it takes to refill my cup is two minutes in a place where I just sit and soak in the beauty, in awe of the view. My sons love the mountains. They are captivated by those snow-capped peaks that linger for most of the year because it's just that cold up there. They love the occasional tiny waterfall or insanely beautiful teal-blue lake which would surface "just around that bend" as we would drive to our destination.

This day was no different than any other—just me and the boys in the mountains, venturing to find that perfect spot. We found a great picnic spot, with picnic benches of course because their momma does not like sitting on the ground. We sat at a picnic table which was more than socially distant (before this was a thing) from the other picnic tables sprinkled across this patch of land, surrounded by a cul-de-sac of mountains, and perched at the edge of a tiny lake. My back was to the parking lot which was a short three-minute walk to our table. We sat in silence; the boys on their iPads, who would soon complain that there was no Wi-Fi, while I stared at The Three Sisters, the mountains that were the backdrop of my wedding day in Canmore years before. Nothing smells greater than fresh mountain spring air on an unseasonably warm day for the time of year. *Gosh, I love it out here*, I thought to myself.

CRACK!

I was jolted out of my mountain trance by a deafening explosion that seemingly came from the back of The Three Sisters range. *What the heck was that? Did a plane crash?* Suddenly, a veil of dark, black smoke curled around the mountain, quickly filling the view. I told the kids to get up! As we ran towards the parking lot, each one of us was able to grab a hand to stick together. We did not scream. We didn't even look back. Everyone else did, but we just hustled to the vehicle. As I fumbled for my keys to unlock the doors, suddenly there was silence. No one was screaming. I looked around the parking lot and no one was there. I quickly looked behind me where the benches were, and everyone was either already back at their picnic table or still walking back. The smoke was gone. I looked at the boys and they seemed unphased. I was disturbed, but I was starting to feel calmer and with that, I had the confidence to go back. After all, everyone else had done it.

We headed back to our table and started to enjoy a wonderful lunch and a laugh. We didn't even speak of what had just happened. The peace was nice, calming, and Zen.

CRACK!

It happened again and as if on repeat, everyone ran to the parking lot, as did the kids and me. The whole sequence happened once more and then I woke up. It was a dream—or a nightmare. At the time, I had no context, but a short two months later, I was about to find out it wasn't just a dream, it was a nightmare.

* * *

After a very dynamic year with an abundance of change, I needed a mom-cation. All the arrangements were made for a post-Mother's Day long weekend visit with my bestie in Toronto. She would still have to work while I was there, which was perfect. I love Toronto and enjoy visiting the city. I love being able to walk with the human tide and no one knows I am from out of town. I love having a mid-afternoon cocktail on the harbour while others are working. This is a vacation to me. The break was needed, and I had a perfect time. I went to the aquarium, walked around downtown, sat on a few patios, had lunch with friends, but mainly I spent time alone. It was a great mom-cation. I finished it off in an overnight stay in a hotel near the airport. I checked in and told the lovely concierge about how I had spent my trip. She was in complete awe. She, too, was a mom and felt more mothers needed to do this. She upgraded my room, of course, and gave me a high five. I had a lovely glass of wine, watched TV, and slept in the comfort of a bed that didn't have four people in it. The next day I checked out, went to the airport, and travelled home.

By the time I landed back home I was feeling stressed. I couldn't understand why I felt this way. My husband picked me up from the airport and we said little to each other. Once we arrived home, and about an hour before we had to pick the kids up from school, he announced that he wanted a divorce. He waited until the day I came back from a vacation, and minutes before I would see my sons, after four days away from them. I was blindsided with untimely disappointment.

Earlier that year, I had left my well-paying job with great benefits and security to be less stressed and more accessible at home. There was no doubt I was a hard worker. I came from an economically starved home, growing up, and I never wanted my kids to experience this.

The man standing across the room from me, demanding a divorce, always knew that and supported the move. My family was everything to me and many transitions were happening in our world. I was ready to live leaner and be more present. Leaving that job was a decision we both made—we both felt it was right. Only a few months later, this was now obviously the wrong choice. He wanted a divorce, which he had wanted for a long time, and there was nothing I could say to change his mind. Even so, I presented several options, from counselling to taking a three-month break. It was clear he had made his decision and had been thinking about it for a while. He wanted to move out that day.

I requested he move to the finished basement and that we could tell the kids a story as to why he was down there. I reasoned that the kids needed to finish the school year before their lives were going to be devastated. While we didn't agree on how the kids would react, I was very clear that I wanted to make sure how and when they were told was well thought out—scripted even—and managed to make sure they got the support they needed. I wanted a therapist set up for them. I wanted members on both sides of our family there when we broke the news. I wanted them to know that they were supported. I also knew that when all these steps were met, we were officially done.

I went to the gym right away. I cried alone in silence every chance I could because I was holding it in when the boys were around. I had to be strong, smart, and wise for my kids. They say women are strong, but mark my words, a mother, when she knows she must be, is one of the strongest people you will ever know—especially when she has told herself there is no other option.

The explosion, the calm, the explosion, calm-and-repeat dream—that was a sign. There are always signs. There are always messages. In that dream, I was in the mountains with my boys. While it was not uncommon for me to be with them doing tons of fun activities it was very unlikely I would have taken a road trip without my husband. That dream was missing a piece and that piece was my husband. The explosion represented a shocking moment that caused major panic and fear (divorce) and then finding my way to calm (being strong for my boys for over a month), then an explosion (telling the boys we were divorcing), then calm again (having all the tools and things set up to help them navigate the storm) and resuming life as close to normal as possible.

I share these two stories to discuss how breakups happen. Many of us feel blindsided, but the signs are always there. Distant behaviour, lying, sneaky actions, basically any uncharacteristic behaviour can be a sign that a breakup is imminent. I don't say this to create fear, but I sense if you are reading this book, you are in the reality of a breakup, not checking to see if you are about to have one.

There are many types of breakups: being blindsided, slow burn, expected or unexpected, separation or divorce. In the most serious cases, it could be caused by infidelity, some sort of emotional, physical, or mental abuse, or perhaps because of substance abuse issues. No two breakups are identical, but there are themes or common factors which typically connect them: communication, finances, and sex. One might dispute that but look at it in another way.

When I Google, "top reason people get divorced," I get around 219 million items to review on this subject. Some of these sites will give a very robust list, others will summarize. Inevitably, all the items on any list will fall under those three categories which we often hear about throughout our relationships/marriage.

First, you must have sex in a relationship. I heard a saying some time ago: "keep your man's belly full and his balls empty if you want to keep him." That is crass, but oddly it rings with some truth. Next on the list: there was too much arguing, he said too many horrible things, or she was always nagging. I put all of that under the category of communication which is a priority in a relationship/marriage. Then it's about finances. If there was a gambling problem, a substance abuse issue, a shopping issue, or the need to "always have new things" issue, all of them lead to financial problems. It all equals maxed out credit cards, lack of savings, and no alignment in spending habits. No matter what you want to believe, this will lead you to a stressful place in your relationship. Sex, communication, finances—these are the most powerful three issues that lead to a breakup.

My divorce was a shocker to me and everyone else. As I shared the news, I received the same instantaneous response over and over. Some were buckled at the knees, driven to limitless tears, or struck by a painfilled silence. Simply put, they were blown away which affirmed my shock. It was as if someone had just been told they had mere months to live. The pain was present in every moment and conversation. Although everyone reacted to their shock differently, it was plagued by the same intensity and remorse.

The questions that came in were like a broken record. "Have you both tried to go to counselling?" "Have you agreed to a trial separation?" The list went on and my answer was always, the same—it is really that simple, we are done, and it is out of my control.

God knows I tried. I begged my husband to try therapy, but he declined with an assurance that told me it was over. I thought that we could work things out. As far as I know, there was no infidelity. According to him, he wanted to take a different path and was convinced that path did not include me. I can still remember the feedback he gave me to this day, and how it made me feel. He felt it was important to let me know he was no longer attracted to me because I had not reached my full potential, and he felt I was blocking him from reaching his full potential. He went on to say that he believed we both had "twin flames" out there for us and he wanted to find his. To top it all off, he said there were just too many *signs* that said we should not be together (e.g., a song frequently playing on the radio). I mean how can you argue with that?

I knew in my heart that the relationship was done, and so much of what was happening was out of my control. He was so strong in his conviction that I convinced myself that even if he woke up and said, "This is a mistake, I want to fix what is broken," there was no turning back. It turns out that thinking about this was a wasted emotion. That day never came. It was over. My heart was broken by the end of this relationship and our family of four, which was everything to me.

It was time for me to move forward. It was time to heal. I didn't want to waste another moment on a man who wasn't committed to me, so rather than deconstruct why the marriage failed, I decided I didn't want to carry the heavy burden of pain. My focus had to be on my children and our future, my future. In this challenge, I found the key to unlocking that future, the key to accelerated healing. Come hell or high water, I was determined to move forward fast.

Let this be your guide to do the same. I've given you practical exercises that helped me release the shackles as quickly as I could so that I could heal. Now it's your turn. It's time to roll up your sleeves and do the work and keep your focus on what you want on the other side of your breakup. I want you to envision who you want to see when you look in the mirror, on the other side of this challenge, and ask yourself how that will feel. That, along with the exercises in this book, will help you move forward and heal from this painful part of your journey.

Real Talk

Were experience a lot of breakups in our lives. I'm taking us back several years to a scene where I learned some heartbreaking news. This was some years before I would meet my future husband. Maybe that's why I remember it like it was yesterday; every vivid detail stuck in my mind.

The day was nothing short of stunning. From the ceremony to the cocktail hour, everything was smooth, well thought out, mindful of the guests, and mesmerizing. The outdoor ceremony had the perfect amount of cloud and sun to manage the heat of the day. The grass could not have been greener in this quaint, but posh, farm-inspired acreage just minutes from the city limits. There was minimal need for decoration because the ambience of the venue already had a modern rustic feel that one need not alter. The bride and groom complimented this with a variety of fresh, seasonal floral arrangements that included tiger lilies, daisies, spider mums, and a variety of other flowers to make each bouquet unique and rustic. The bride wore a simple, but very elegant nonrestrictive mermaid gown. The groom wore a warm grey suit which at the time was rare. He had a pale-yellow tie with a white shirt. Both bride and groom only had two attendants each, making it even more simple and memorable. Once the ceremony was done, they were whisked off for pictures.

We, the guests, had assigned tables that were decorated just as simply as the rest of the wedding. The newlyweds truly looked happy, and we were all happy for them. I am rarely good at hiding my emotions. I do not have a poker face. As they entered the room and we jumped and clapped, I felt an instant wave of jealousy. I wondered whether this would ever happen for me or if I was doomed to have failed relationships. After all, I was good at breakups, or so it seemed.

The drinks were flowing, and we were all laughing, drinking, and being merry. After a lot of dancing, a group of old friends sat around a table tackling some much-needed late-night snacks. We were all bantering back and forth. I can't even remember what the setup was, but the response from one of my friends was, "Yeah, it's like how Sarah and Mike are sleeping together behind Carli's back." The table turned cold and silent. This part I remember. This part was clear. For some reason, I did a quick scan of the table. At the time, I felt I did it to get a "just joking" glance from someone. Nothing. Here's what I did see. Faces that were not shocked by this news. Faces that were pissed that I just found out this way. Faces that were embarrassed for me. Faces that had no clue what to do.

As I locked eyes with the girl who dropped this incredibly awkward truth bomb, I saw a face that succumbed to instant regret. Somehow, I could see through the regret in the way it was delivered to a deeper truth that she felt this was something I needed to know. Time stood still. Before I could react, I was swiftly taken outside by one of the girls. Good thing she did that because before I knew it, I was vomiting profusely. I felt like it was never going to stop. I wish it were the liquor, but it was not. It was my body reacting to the most devastating adult moment I was about to face at that time. At 24 years old, I just found out my absolute best friend in the entire world, the one with whom I shared ridiculous highs and lows in life, had been sleeping with the man I had been madly in love with for over four years. In one quick swoop, two relationships I valued more than most were being put in front of a mental juror.

It was one of the most challenging, devastating, confusing moments, and I do not wish that type of embarrassment, shame, or painful, undignified moment on anyone. The moment that you are told something like that, you would hope that someone would have the decency to tell you before in private, but instead, they allow you to experience it this way. It wasn't right at all, but it was real, and I had to face the raw emotions it brought up.

I spent the next day, the next week, the next month, and the next year in a similar space. Alone, depressed, broken, and more. My friends were socially distancing from me before it was cool because I was unpleasant, negative, bitchy, and bitter to be around. There was no openness to listen to my feelings. I was living in a "get over it" environment. However, I didn't know how to get over it. My feelings were overwhelming and real. I felt I had no reconciliation from that moment. There was no sound person around who could give me great advice to navigate this. So, I chose to do what no person should do. I wasted over a year in a pity party for one that nobody would want to join if I let them. I hated my body. I hated my circumstances. I hated being so alone. I was like the walking dead. I was living my life on autopilot. This was my routine: get up, get dressed, do my makeup, go to work, go home, repeat. Not much more. I went out occasionally, faked a smile but lacked any trust for anyone,

 25

and felt unseen. In one fell swoop, I found myself mourning for an entire year. That was it. I woke up and said fuck it, I'm not spending another minute in this place.

I choose to share this story because there is no way that I want you to have to experience that. It is fundamentally why I used every ounce of my energy to make sure I did not go back to that practice when I was faced with the most painful breakup, divorce. Well, more painful because it meant yet another broken family in what seemed to be a systemic problem on both sides of our family, something I was so adamant not to repeat. It was painful because I felt, at the time that I had failed my kids, and that stings like nothing else.

What I learned from the first situation that later gave me tools (because everything is a lesson) to face the divorce, was one clear thing. Time wasted in the "pity pool party" is wasted time. People may stop by to check out the party, realize that sad music is playing, the shitty snacks are unhealthy, there is a Charlie Brown cloud overhead, and no one (you) is pleasant to be around. So, they leave promptly, and you are still left at this party until one day you realize you, too, are not having fun. I learned, in other words, that you waste time, you make unhealthy choices, you alienate yourself from others, and you essentially create a space no one deserves to be in.

So, it's time to get out of the pool. Stop wasting your precious commodity – time. It's time to get out of bed, release the anger, live a life of peace, be happy, and move forward.

Are you with me? Good. Here is some real talk that's going to move you forward. You have *one* damn life! Say it out loud: *I*

have one damn life! A life of pain, loss, transitions, maybe even health challenges. You have been in the fire without a fire extinguisher. You have been hurt. You will get through this. If you were raised in a challenging environment or landed in one all on your own, you have been trained to face this scene in your play. You are a gladiator. If you were sheltered and coddled, you probably watched enough television or read enough books to be familiar with stories of perseverance. You admired from a distance what others went through and sat there in awe of the performances you saw on TV. The thing is, this is your scene, and you are not getting a dress rehearsal. There will be no table script readings, no direction on how the scene should play out. This scene will be the hardest to get through, but when you finish, you will win all the accolades of the people around you. You will inspire others. You will be the person who people come to and beg you to help them be like you. *You will be that person.* But you need to listen up and listen intently. Remember, you are having one damn life. This is your time and your moment. So, to start the process of reassuring you that I am here, I want you to know:

You are not to blame. You should not be ashamed. You are not being punished. You are not a victim. You did not will this to happen. You are a good person. You are not the first to go through this. You will be able to live again. You are loved!

This is a start—the start of our journey together. These are affirmative statements that can help us through this process, that will also help when you are back (only for a moment) in a place that may not serve you, such as:

- You will get caught up in retracing your steps.
- You will want to identify every moment you might have messed up.
- You will relive the crap you put up with.

That person is not you and you are not them! They have their line in the sand, and you have yours. You might have moved that line several times, but you do have a line; it was just never reached. So, retracing steps, reliving every detail is not going to help. Honestly, if you are female, by default you are more accommodating, more adaptable, and more flexible. You are also one who will heal properly and grow from this experience. The odds are in your favour.

You also did not bring this upon yourself. Maybe your relationship ended because of financial challenges—no one wills this. When I discuss willing something into your life, I mean there are books and information out there about the law of attraction. That is where we are told that we have somehow willed everything and anything that has happened in our lives. I believe in that to a certain extent, but I think there are more details in that message that many are not communicating. You did not want to be heartbroken, but maybe you were hoping for changes in your spouse that conflicted with what they were willing for themselves. That could be a thing. Maybe your relationship ended because of poor communication or a poor sex life—no one consciously wills this either. To be in alignment with one another we need to be able to connect through our words. We must as a couple, be invested in growing together, elevating each other, but when one checks out it is damn hard to do the work on your own to get him or her to check back in.

People change, but not always the way we want them to or expect them to. I heard a judge on TV once talking about her 25-year marriage. She was asked how it had been successful for that long. She replied that because who they were at five years into the marriage was not the same as who they were at ten years and 25 years. She went on to say that she would be lying if she said that they had been prepared for each other's changes and transitions, but they were committed to making it work. They were both invested in each other and did not see an easy exit. Yes, divorce or breakup preparations are easy exits. It is tough to navigate through a challenge instead of avoiding it, checking out, and hoping it goes away. If the relationship has a healthy foundation but hits a rough patch, you find common ground and work it out. If it is unhealthy, then yes, it is probably best to exit.

So, what does this have to do with willing things into our lives? Well, in marriage we make vows, right? In those vows, we say, "I plan to honour you, cherish you, etc." Another part of the vows is "for better or for worse, for richer or poorer, etc." In other words, we vow when we marry that we plan to and are willing to manage the highs and lows. This includes uncomfortable changes. We aim to work more on the positive stuff (for better, for richer), but relationships are not easy and some of us get an abundance of for worse, and for poorer.

However, we also find out if we are truly okay with that. I know people who came from wealthy families, who married "for poorer" but are genuinely happy. I know the opposite as well, people who came from humble beginnings and married wealthy but are miserable. I know that people do not know what their line in the sand is until they are there. Most of us never actually talk about it either. The point is, one or both of you, intentionally willed positivity into your relationship, but you also willed the potential for challenges. However, when the challenges come, they increasingly put stress on your relationship. No one wants darkness in their relationships, but like day and night, it is inevitable. You will have challenging moments. Some you deal with; many you dust under the rug hoping they will go away. They do not. If you keep dusting things under the rug, eventually there is no more room for things under that rug. You are then faced with dealing with them. The outcome is not always great. But when someone checks out of the relationship, the rug they were dusting things under probably filled up faster than yours, and they probably didn't want to deal with it anymore. This is just speculation. As I said, everyone has a line in the sand.

Couples also do not know how they will manage a challenge until they face it. They do not always know if when life throws them lemons, they even like lemonade, until they are forced to do something with the dang lemons life has thrown at them. Challenges, and how we navigate them, are the one true test of character and integrity. Will you hurt others because you cannot manage your own pain? Will you try to crush others because you are crushed? Will you keep secrets from someone else until you have your plans figured out, only to hurt them in the process and blindside them? No! But people do. Heck, it might have been you who did this to someone else. More than likely, if you are reading this book, your spouse probably did you dirty. That is why you are reading this book.

Stop the negative self-talk—the cognitive loop playing in your head over and over—the one telling you that you are not

good enough. You are not worthy. You messed up. You are a failure. You are ashamed. You did not do this. You did not do that. Stop the chatter in your head. It is not serving you; it is only exacerbating the problem. You are good enough, you are smart enough, and you are worthy enough of everything you deserve (which is better than what has happened). You did not mess up. You are the furthest thing from a failure (even though failure is a good thing because we grow from it). You have absolutely nothing to be ashamed of. Combat those negative thoughts by instantly turning them around and align them with who you are. You are a good person.

You might never fully know what caused the breakup. If there was an affair, you might never know what led your partner to indulge in that temptation. If there was financial betrayal, you might never know why your partner thought they could get rich from a potential quick-win situation that ended up destroying your family. If it was a lack of healthy communication, you might never know why your ex wasn't willing to find the words to work through your problems.

You might question if they ever loved you at all. Do not question it, and do not give it another thought. If those thoughts creep up, let them go and release them to God.

When you are healing you find sources of comforting information everywhere. Of course, you must be careful that they are not soothing dark stuff that will create more problems for you. One day, I stumbled across a video from Elevation Church. Pastor Steven Furtick, who I didn't even know existed until my divorce, was pictured on the video with the title "When the battle chooses you." Even though it took an hour to watch,

I felt it was good to press play and so I did. The focus of this sermon was about how you do not choose a battle, it chooses you, and what you do about it. This is an important place to end this chapter.

There will be times, like with me, when I wanted to rest and not think about who did what or what I was supposed to do. I was accommodating, but I also tried to understand. I stood my ground when I needed to and advocated for myself. But I didn't think I ever would have chosen to marry someone who would choose to not fight for us. That choice was made without my consent. The battle, as anyone can imagine after a divorce with kids, is a flipping struggle; one I did not choose. However, someone else's challenges are not mine. I can help as much as I can, but I cannot control someone else's moves. That video was a reminder. I must know when the battle is mine. Once I realize that it is not, I must let it go and turn to healing, not to fighting something outside of what I can control. I had to release it, take a step forward, and move away from it.

EXERCISE

"In three words I can sum up everything I have learned about life: it goes on."

- ROBERT FROST

To create awareness to help you to reconnect with a world that is moving forward, answer the following questions:

1. Who in your life has had a challenge and you've watched them move forward as if nothing happened? How do you think they did that? What were some of the things you witnessed?

2. What have you gone through and yet somehow managed to rise from the ashes? What were some of the ways you got through it? What can you do to incorporate those strategies again?

3. When you are on the other side of this struggle, what would you like your life to look like? Do you see a new relationship? What would the person and the relationship look like? Dream! Is it a certain success? What would that look like?

Breaking up Is Hard to Do

In 2006, I went through a challenging time. I was in a job that was unbelievably taxing. It was 100 per cent commission, I had already given two years of my life to it, and I was barely making $40,000 (before tax) at the time. Yes, I was single, but the cost of living was increasing, I was still paying off an exceptionally large student loan debt, and I was behind on my bills. I was living on my own with the usual expenses: rent, electricity, insurance, as well as all of life's necessities. I was increasingly scared and deflated. When your goals and dreams seem out of reach, it is extremely hard to keep moving forward. I thought that because I had sacrificed moving up in my previous job (this has never really been a motivator for me) for the land of potential riches, this was supposed to be *the* job that would reward me. Unfortunately, I was two years in with no reward. I was close to a breakthrough, but I was not quite there yet. The experience was demoralizing. Moves like that are hard and not for the faint of heart. To separate yourself from people to follow your dreams is isolating, lonely, and challenging, however, when you work that hard most people cannot understand, and most people can't help. You just want to be better and to have the money to play with your friends (e.g., trips, buy great stuff, and feel good). Sounds superficial, but it's true.

I wanted to travel, but dreams like that only could be accomplished with money. Keep in mind, this was before travel blogs were a thing—it was difficult to find out how to travel with next to nothing. I watched as my friends took travel vacations, enjoyed nights out, and there I was hustling and burning out quickly, all for what seemed like nothing. I could tell my boss was getting annoyed with my "great potential, but inconsistent results." News flash: so was I. The best people for jobs like this are those with a great work ethic, zero fear of going into debt, or who have parents to call on to help them out. I only had a great work ethic and while I could perform well under pressure, financially, I just wasn't where I needed to be.

I was lucky to find a part-time job, something my full-time boss did not like. He felt if I just put more time into my current role, I would break the barrier holding me back. All I thought was, *I don't have time for that shit, I need more money, today*. The part-time role was at a small pub about ten blocks from work. It was hard to take this on because even though I know that making extra money is smart, I was becoming well-known in my profession, and I risked losing credibility by having that part-time job. Wearing a suit during the day and an apron in the evening confuses people. There is no shame in the apron. Shoot, I made more money in an evening than I did in four days at my other job. But perception is what it is; people judge and would wonder about my professional path. At least, that is what I thought at the time. I really wanted to be successful and at that moment I was feeling exceptionally low.

The pub serviced regulars, for the most part, mainly men, who were there so often you knew their schedules. There was a group who were there every day after work. There was a group that only came on Fridays. They were usually not the most polished-looking people and just came to unwind after a busy week in a labour job. Others came on Saturday nights for wings, beer, and other pub activities (e.g., darts, slots, trivia).

Working in this profession is not easy, especially when you have a day job. And I worked hard. Between waiting on tables, I was restocking the coolers, doing my own bartending, bussing tables, and I had to clean the bathrooms at the end of the night. I had no other life because it was all work for me. Eventually, people at the pub became my friends, and one of them became a love interest.

The group of guys who came in the pub on Friday or Saturday nights—hardworking types, but rough around the edges, were unbelievably nice to me and were always keeping an eye out for me (in case someone was being a jerk). As I'm sure you can imagine, I started to connect with one of them. There was something there, but I don't like to mix business with pleasure, so I never made a move. He didn't either. Although I clicked with the guy, nothing happened at first. I could say it was because he was not my type, but I do not have a type—no two guys I dated were alike, at least visually.

One night, the pub was busier than normal. We had only three people working, the owner, the cook, and me. The perk was that if I survived that night, I would make a killing in tips. We were backed up with people waiting for orders. I was a satisfactory server at best. I had a good memory which served me well, but I had a challenging time when the pub was up to capacity. The owner and I were hustling, and suddenly something I did upset him. This turned into a yelling match in front of the customers, and I abruptly quit the job. It was embarrassing because the owner yelled at me in front of everyone. When I stuck up for myself, he said, "If you don't like it, you can fuck off!" So, I did. I guess I was fired. It was humiliating, to say the least, but he was who he was, and I too was unhappy.

One of the regulars, who I will call Hailey, had become a friend. Shortly after the incident at the pub, we ran into each other in an office building close to my day job. We hugged and briefly chatted. She mentioned her birthday was coming up and she was celebrating at that same pub. She also told me the owner was incredibly sad about how things ended and that others at the pub wanted to see me. At that point, I was missing my pub friends since I had distanced myself from my real friends to pursue my career and make money.

Hailey's party was on a Friday night. I was nervous to go because it was the first time I'd been there since the fight. The guy (l will call him Will) and his friends were there, like clockwork, playing their weekly game of trivia. We ended up hanging out the entire night and were inseparable from that night on. While it was fun at first, it didn't take long to learn that this relationship wasn't healthy. It was completely one-sided. When we went out with people, it was only with his friends. I had met all the people in his life, and I knew all about his work, but when the opportunity arose for him to meet my friends at an upcoming event, he froze and said he didn't want to go. When I asked why he stated that he wasn't ready. Huh? *But I know all the people in his life*, I thought. The relationship went downhill from there. Our daily conversations turned into weekly conversations. We both were filling in time.

On the first day of spring, I realized we needed to do something. I texted him and asked if we could talk. He agreed and I called. I asked him what was going on. He said he wasn't sure, but he felt there was supposed to be more to the relationship. I could tell he just wanted the problem (me) to go away, but he wouldn't say it. Instead, I said, "It's spring. Let's start spring cleaning." Super cheesy, I know, but I've never been good at ending relationships. He agreed and we were now officially over, though we hadn't seen each other for a couple of weeks. I got off the phone and cried, though I'm not sure why; probably from all the stress and the fact that I hate breaking up with people. It's just uncomfortable. One minute you are so connected to someone and the next, you don't want anything to do with them. It's so strange. I completely get why people wait to have sex because within three to six months the truth will surface—you will either want to be together or want nothing to do with one another. It only takes six months, maximum.

The point is, breakups are hard, especially when you know that the other person has decided and doesn't respect you enough to say something. While all breakups suck, let's be clear that most breakups aren't mutual. One of you has given up and the other has gone along with it. After all, what can you do if someone does not want to be with you? Begging only works temporarily. Quite honestly, if breakups were mutual, we would see way more social media posts with people arm-in-arm in front of the courthouse, gleefully getting a divorce, or former couples attending the same barbeque or singing songs around a campfire, but that is rare.

In relationships, we invest time. We meet someone, find them interesting, and give them the most valuable item in our lives, time. And yet, when we make these decisions, we don't protect our time by doing some due diligence in the beginning. At the end of a breakup, how many of us have thought, "Did I see the signs?" Lord knows you have that one friend—or two—who have no problem telling you how the person was all wrong for you and that they saw 1,000 things wrong with them. Insert eye roll. So, when we break up with someone, we have essentially lost an investment. However, we have gained something better. We have gained knowledge, experience, and awareness.

As a woman who has recovered from many breakups and has helped many friends through breakups, I have noticed that we wallow. We throw pity parties, we cry, we whine, we say, "Woe is me." We are disappointed in the breakup, even when we know it is the right thing to do. The well-known motivational speaker, John C. Maxwell says, "Disappointment is the gap that exists between expectations and reality," and our expectations, especially once we enter a relationship, are too cloudy to see the potential realities. When you wallow, you do self-destructive things like binge-eat ice cream and chips. You end up gaining the "Relationship 20." Mortified, you buy a gym pass, work out for six months, and lose weight. You might need another six months to emotionally prepare for dating again. Did you know that the average guy, after a divorce, is in a serious relationship within 12 months? This is about the time a woman might just be ready to move on. So right now, I want you to ask yourself, "What the hell are you doing?" Stop bingeing, stop wallowing, and stop whining. Turn off the TV. Put down the phone. Put yourself in a position where you are probably not going to think about it (i.e., attend a paint night with friends, or go to a busy place where you are more focused on people watching or go anywhere that doesn't trigger those memories). I know it sucks and I want to whine too, but it gets us nowhere. Help yourself by making a 21-day whine-free commitment.

All this is hard, I know it is, but when you wallow, you are not living. You are allowing time, that precious commodity, to pass you by. Your ex likely moved on while you've stood still. Why? They won't come back to you, and even if they do, it's probably for a late-night rendezvous (if you catch my drift). This isn't something you truly want. You don't want to get tangled up in one-night stands with an ex. It's pretty much a demotion with only a five, maybe ten-minute benefit. Yes, there are some clear signs at the beginning, but we mostly ignore them out of lust and the feelings of the moment. There is nothing wrong with that if you take away what you have learned. How have you grown? What did you appreciate about the experience? What are the great memories you would like to cherish?

EXERCISE

This is where we take a step back to move forward. Take a moment to answer the following questions. This exercise may make you emotional and that's a good thing. After all, "Tears are not the pain, they are the healing." (Annette Goodheart)

1. When you first realized you liked your ex, what attracted you to him or her? Think qualities, values, traits.

2. What were some of the great things that you learned by being with them? Maybe it was learning a new skill or getting over a fear. For example, I had a horrible boyfriend who once told me, "To help your career, you should be able to hold a three-minute conversation on any topic, at any time." He was right, and I have given that advice to hundreds of people.

3. What were some things that you experienced while being with them? Maybe it was surfing, travelling, or a shared hobby.

Now that you have answered these questions, look at your answers and realize that everything here is transferable. The qualities and traits you liked are transferable. You can take this list and add the things you might like to have or experience in your next relationship. Even beyond romantic relationships, what you have learned will be valuable for the rest of your life.

Even if it seems negative, it isn't. If it is something you wouldn't do again, then great, now you know. The experiences that you had with this person are also transferable to your everyday life. You can still surf, you can still travel.

Grief

*"If you don't grieve right,
you won't heal right."*

~ Pastor Sheryl Brady

I will never forget that day. It was sunny and warm outside, at the end of my Grade Nine school year. It was not a great year for me—midway through the year, I was kicked out of the school I had attended since Grade Four. I found myself in a new school, an outsider just a few months short of Grade Nine graduation. Although many faces were familiar as I had gone to elementary school with many of the kids, I felt rejected. I guess to them I looked like bad news. I could see the labels in their eyes. Look at that poor, thug girl. It looks like she never takes a shower. It didn't help that within two to three weeks of attending that school, I stepped in someone's puke in front of a lot of students who were waiting for some clueless idiot to do just that. I was making the wrong friends. To top it off, I got chicken pox just weeks before the actual grad ceremony, which I was beyond brave to attend—as I was going alone covered from head to toe in dried-out chicken pox scabs. Not my finest moment. But the fun was only beginning that year. A massive shake-up was coming, and it was all beyond my control.

The day started with a lot of tension, although I'm not sure what was driving it that day. Our home was a blended family—a bi-racially blended family in the late 80s, early 90s. There were five kids in our home and two adults. This was not the first home we had together though. In the six-plus years we lived together this was probably home number seven. We moved a lot, and we were always on pins and needles. The house was filled with teenagers, all with different personalities, barely functioning in a very unstable environment with no space to breathe. What did people think? That we would be happy? We never knew if we were going to get three meals in a day or if the electricity was going to be cut off until "help came through," whatever that meant. So, while the atmosphere that day was tense, in many ways it started like any other day. It was a day when anything could happen, and we wouldn't be surprised—except for this.

My dad and his wife were arguing savagely. I can't remember what the argument was about, all I knew was that it was loud and scary. This wasn't good. This was going to be harsh. I fled the house with one of my siblings. When I came back two or three hours later, the house was calm, but it was also basically empty. She was gone and so were her children. My dad sat alone at the table. I looked around—there was no one. The closets were empty, half of the living room furniture was gone, and we were left with big gaping spaces where people and their belongings once resided. Instant emptiness. An instant obliteration of seven years of a blended family, stories, investments, and shared experiences.

While it hadn't been perfect, it was something and without warning, I was abandoned once again, with no chance to say

goodbye. I felt discarded and it hurt like hell. I was once again being asked to carry a burden I was too young to carry, and the baggage brought with it a mix of emotions that were irrational, heartbreaking, and unkind. Where was the comfort for me? Who would help me reconcile my pain? Who could I call?

I began to move through the stages of grieving the loss of my imperfect, blended family. My rebelliousness amplified and I was kicked out of school in Grade Ten. I didn't care because it felt like no one cared about me. No adult pulled me aside and said, "I got you and will help you get through this." Instead, I was told, "Get over it and suck it up." At the tender age of 14, I was hormonal as heck, living in a very unstable home environment, suffering from malnutrition, and treated like a write-off from the school system. This was too much to navigate for someone that age.

I share this story because breakups and grief take many forms but there is something they have in common. They are never easy, and they hurt like hell. Of course, the most common ending is grief triggered by death. While I don't mean to downplay the agony brought on by death, there are often different parameters and support systems in death. Often people come together when someone dies. Funerals, flowers, and house gatherings occur after a death. There is support, shoulders to cry on, phone calls, frequent check-ins. In the case of a divorce or breakup, much of that is lacking, especially when no logic or explanation is provided. It's a loss most people don't seem to know how to approach. They feel bad, but they need answers. Did he cheat? Did she cheat? Did he gamble their money away? Were they fighting all the time? This was not my experience. The community may have come together sporadically for occasions, but they did not come directly to me. I could go to their house as the door was open, and yet with death, they come to you. Both are instances of grief. Both have been measured to be the equivalent of each other in terms of potential individual psychological damage. However, in the eyes of many, family breakups still allow for mobility to travel, to reach out, to ask for support. Death does not. I'm not sure about the logic behind that, but it seems to be the case.

I am going to take you on the journey of grief. Some may be familiar with it, some may not. I am doing this not just to identify what you may find on the Internet, but to help you thoroughly understand each stage, as I have experienced it with multiple breakups, including the divorce and divorces I went through as a child that impacted me. Let's dive in.

Grief is caused by a loss. It could surface with the loss of a loved one, but it can also occur for many other reasons. It could be due to the loss of a family member by death or abandonment, or it could be the loss of an older sister's boyfriend who was like a big brother to you when they broke up. Either is a loss. Grief could result from the loss of an influential and caring teacher who changed schools and was never to be seen again. It could be caused by the loss of a cherished item that accidentally made its way down a drainpipe somewhere. It is still a loss. Grief can surface at any time, however, there is very intense grief and less intense grief. The latter is something relatively easy to get over, such as losing your favourite shirt. Yes, you may always think about it, but it is relatively easy to find a satisfying replacement with some good retail therapy. When you lose a loved one to death or a divorce/breakup, the intensity of the grief will make you navigate very concrete, but haphazard stages because no two people navigate grief the same way.

There are different stages of grief, the most acknowledged being the five stages of grief discovered and introduced to the world by Elisabeth Kübler-Ross in her book *On Death and Dying* in 1969. Her work was also adopted and built upon by David Kessler who has several books and readily available information online. The five stages of grief are:

- Denial
- Anger
- Bargaining
- Depression
- Acceptance

Before we dive in, I have a disclaimer. I am not a licensed professional. I have had many life experiences but am not a professional psychiatrist. I choose to refer to who I believe is the number one leader on this subject. David Kessler worked with Elisabeth Kübler-Ross on two books before she passed away. He has written more, and he is a multiple best-selling author. I encourage you to connect with his books and resources to learn more. He discusses all types of grief from death to job loss to divorce. I am just scratching the surface here with what I reference and want to keep the integrity of this book focused on the experiences I have lived through.

Denial

Kessler says that this is a stage where you "cannot believe this is happening." You may communicate this verbally or indirectly, but it is obvious that you are in shock. Some people will constantly say this out loud as they navigate tears and numbness.

47

While others, on the outside, will be doing things such as going back to work immediately or going shopping and acting as if nothing happened. The reason for the latter of the two, I believe, is that if you force yourself to do the normal things, you don't have to face the reality of the one missing piece.

I have been on both sides of denial. I went to the gym at 5:00 a.m. the day after my ex-husband announced he wanted a divorce. Other times, I just sat there staring at a wall, as I did when doctors were not optimistic about the viability of a pregnancy, and I was faced with a daunting decision to proceed with tests. I can see now that both times I was in denial and was navigating them the best way I could at the time. The most common denial I have seen is the one that is glorified on movies and TV shows: the girl was dumped by the boy and lays her head on her mom's lap crying, saying, "I can't believe he did this to me," and the mom consoles her with comforting words, or a story she never thought she would have to share, and reminders that she will get through this. What a glorious vision—all that support—but not a situation I have ever experienced.

Denial can be healthy. One minute you could be talking to your partner about being together forever, particularly if you exchanged vows. Only days before, you're professing how you would never hurt one another that way, then they leave a day or two later. No wonder you are in denial, it's a completely valid feeling.

Anger

Now this one is my jam! Not in the sense that I'm enthusiastic about being angry, rather more in terms of self-awareness. I have had to work like hell to learn how to manage this stage and I am happy I consciously made that decision. I grew up in intense instability, suffered while navigating a foundation of abandonment, instability, economic hardship, and at times, emotional starvation. Add in puberty, and I was a rage machine in my teens. It took me until I was in my early 20s to address anger to help better manage it.

Kessler has stated that anger is pretty much your "why phase." This stage typically follows denial and while in it, you will want to know why. "Why did they leave me?" "Why would they hurt me this way?" This stage was tough for me because heavy emotions surfaced, and I tend to get into a mindset in which I feel no one has answers or solutions. While in this stage, I might be out having a good time, and I act up because alcohol will fuel those feelings. By the time I was going through the divorce, I had learned not to do this anymore, but in my 20s rage, being drunk was an outlet and one that probably led to a few broken friendships. In another context, you might randomly throw your coffee mug across the room when a sudden surge of energy comes over you. This might occur while you are grocery shopping, and you stop mid-shop and walk away from a half-full cart. (I witnessed this one in a Costco once—yikes!) You might start to drop friends because they are overly focused on "their problems" and you cannot hear them complaining about shit, so you tell them off and walk away. You may get too agitated with your children over something small which you cannot control and before you know it, you are yelling at them or mocking them when they are upset. I will not lie, this happened once with my oldest child which resulted in both of us crying in each other's arms as we apologized and confessed what we both did wrong. He was ten at the time.

Anger shows up in many ways and it is, in my eyes, one of the unhealthiest of the five stages (next to depression). This is a place where many people get stuck and can't move on and they allow their lives to be temporarily or permanently destroyed. Why does this happen? I feel it is because of that word right there—why. I think people get stuck in the "why." Maybe accompany that word with "how"—and you go on re-peat rotation, constantly reliving situations without coming out with a plan to move out and seek resources to help. Anger is unhealthy because holding onto it can alienate you from others. It can ruin friendships. It can cause you to do very destructive things (e.g., having such a terrible fight with a friend that you never speak to each other again). Anger is just toxic. But it is also very, very, very normal.

One of my children has a behavioural coach. This coach taught us about the anger iceberg. You can google this. It is a picture of an iceberg. There is the part above the water, which is the smallest part of the iceberg. There is the part below the water, which is typically three times the size of what you see of the iceberg. If you have never seen an iceberg in real life, I will tell you they are spectacular and the size of high-rise buildings. That is the part you see. It is overwhelming to know that below you when you are on a boat near an iceberg, is three times what you see. Very powerful! The anger iceberg is labelled—on top, anger. But the image below the surface of the water is all the aspects of anger that are the true root of the problem. The list includes:

- Embarrassment
- Annoyed
- Offended
- Attacked
- Rejected
- Disgusted
- Scared
- Guilt
- Alone
- Grief
- Shame
- Pressured
- Overwhelmed
- Grumpy
- Helpless
- Nervous
- Jealous
- Sad
- And more

Understanding this will help you begin the process to move through it. You can move through this phase, but you must use tools and practice using these tools. In my experience, anger and depression are not easy to navigate without them.

Bargaining

The most impactful bargaining story I ever heard was, "The Parable of the Mustard Seed." There are quite a few versions of this story online, but it should not be confused with the one

51

linked to the Bible. In short, this story is about a mother whose young son dies suddenly and tragically. She searches for ways to revive him. She ends up in front of Buddha or "a wise man," depending on which version you read. She begs this person to bring her son back to life. He knows they can't do this, so he finds an alternative solution without her knowing. She is tasked with going from door to door in her village, telling her story, and seeking one mustard seed from a home that has never experienced loss. As she ventures through this journey, some homes offer her a mustard seed, but she cannot take it because the home is not without grief or loss. She realizes that her story has been helping others navigate their grief and hearing others' stories helped her come to terms with her grief. Now, this is not the polished version of the story, just a brief condensed version. The takeaway here is her obsessive drive to bargain for her son's life. We have all done this after a breakup that crushed us. We bargained somehow, some way, with the person as well as internally to repair the relationship. Some have done so successfully, most of us not so much. Bargaining is the "what if," the stage where we find ourselves seeking alternatives to the reality of the breakup.

Typically, I navigate this one alone, internally. I don't stay in this stage for long, but I do revisit it often during intense grieving periods. I have gone through, "What if I wasn't so focused on being accountable and mature? That person would have stayed." Or "What if I never asked a friend to investigate my crush's feelings for me? Would they have stayed apart? And would I have ended up with my crush instead?" (This happened to me three times before I turned 22 years old. Who knew friends would betray you this way? But also, silly me.)

This is one stage that reminds me of the importance of community and especially support groups. Rabbi Harold S. Kushner discusses the power of support groups in his book *Why Bad Things Happen to Good People*. I have read this amazing book twice to help me navigate grief and loss. Support groups may not be common in your area, so ensure that you have friends and a therapist who can really help.

Depression

The fourth stage is depression. I first want to mention how this is a normal part of the grieving process. Many people feel this word and think they cannot go there, but it is probably inevitable. Depression, oddly enough, shows up in many ways and is far more common than you might think. It is synonymous with grieving. You feel down and may struggle to want to shower, get dressed, or even get out of bed. You may feel the need to binge-eat or binge-watch TV or both. You may avoid people by not returning calls and text messages. And even if you do return them, you give excuses as to why you are not able to attend a function or meetup.

I remember New Year's Eve 2019. I was home alone and had already requested that a friend be open to a call from me if need be. "I don't know what's wrong," I said, "but I think I am depressed." She understood, demonstrated normal amounts of compassion, and we agreed we would touch base no matter what. While I had done all the things that should have helped me manage the year ahead, I had completely forgotten about New Year's Eve.

As a family, we didn't do crazy, wild things, but we still were together. For the first time in 13 years—ten as a family with kids—I was alone, in my house. It was dreadfully quiet and strange. I didn't have an invitation to go anywhere; I didn't have any family checking in on me. It was the first one of "the firsts" post-divorce which I didn't proactively plan. I realized this when it was, frankly, too late. I ended up on the phone with my friend shortly after I stopped banging my head on my bedroom floor to try to stop the crying. My head hit the floor so hard I am surprised I didn't get a headache at the least, and a concussion at the most. It was an intense moment. I thought to myself, *he wanted the divorce. What fucking monster takes a woman's kids from her when he wanted to leave the family?* I am being honest. I was overwhelmed, full of diverse emotions: anger, frustration, sadness, and pain. I didn't prepare for this at all, as best as I could under the circumstances anyway, and the evening could have ended up much worse. These emotions were overwhelming—I felt as if I was reliving the day that I was dumped. It wasn't the breakup at this point; it was the loss of family.

By this point, most people on his side had stopped talking to me. Only two people reached out to me. I also was struggling with the realization that I was now a contributor to the systemic problems that plagued both sides of my family. Divorce was a sick curse on both sides of the fence, and I was shocked to find myself contributing to that, even if it hadn't been my choice. All these thoughts came crashing over me at that moment, and I found myself on the floor. When I look back, I know that I did many other things to help myself get through, and I was probably hoping I could bypass this one. I was hyper-vigilant about proactively checking the boxes. Everyone says the first year is the most difficult, especially all the first occasions: Christmas, Halloween, Easter, and birthdays. But New Year's Eve—it snuck up on me and hit me like a ton of bricks.

As I disclosed, I am not a therapist, and while I am going to provide several tips to help you in this area later in the chapter, I am unable to close out this section without giving you at least one. I highly recommend you reach out to a therapist or a trusted friend and tell them what is going on. Talking this out is critical, and even more so, it is crucial to know you have support. My bestie was there, on the phone, during my New Year's Eve meltdown. I was so flipping scared, but she was there, albeit thousands of miles away with a new baby, but she was there, nonetheless. I am forever grateful for that moment of support.

Acceptance

COVID-19 has burned into our mind the term: "new normal." Acceptance is essentially coming to terms with your new normal, post-breakup. It doesn't mean that you are perfectly fine with everything that has happened. It doesn't mean that you are OK with the loss of your relationship. It is that your relationship has ended, and you now know you will move on and survive. That is acceptance, at least the best way I can describe it. You have been able to accept that this loss is still a loss, but that you will rise above it and live your life. I hit this stage the moment we told the kids. We had waited to tell the kids, and I knew that for me, in that time if nothing had changed, this separation was final. I guess you could say I went from bargaining to denial, to acceptance—I thought—and then later, anger and depression. My emotional process for the divorce was a lattice that looked like a complicated roller-coaster ride.

Many twists and turns and surprises.

While I have put these in a specific order, please know that grief is not linear. At any given time, you can be in one stage and quickly move to another—and then back. I love this quote from Vicki Harrison who says, "Grief is like the ocean. It comes on in waves, ebbing and flowing. Sometimes the water is calm, and sometimes it is overwhelming. All we can do is learn to swim."

Even when you go through the entire cycle, which may not be in any way, you could be triggered a year later and revisit one of the stages of grief.

Section 2:

Healing - Mind, Body, and Soul

"A person once said, don't be afraid to start over again. This time, you're not starting from scratch, you are starting from experience."

~ Anonymous

Starting Over, Again

As I mentioned in the last chapter, we cycle through grief every time we experience a breakup. The difference is that you now have the strength and the life lessons from previous experiences to help you through. Looking back at my divorce, I got through the first few months after my husband announced he was leaving me, on an adrenaline high. My first focus was on my kids. Step one was to set them up for success before I could truly begin my process of healing and moving forward.

My kids, at that point, did not know we were separating. I was on this high of activating and activity—everything in me knew I had to get things together fast to get things under control. To get myself under control. The first course of action was that he, stay put. I was adamant that he did not move out that day (as he planned to do) and to move to the basement. We would just explain to the kids that it was too hot in the house and their dad was more comfortable in the basement. However, as stated before, my oldest son was way smarter than that. Especially since my soon-to-be ex-husband not only packed everything up in bins right away but filled the spare room he was staying in with his stuff. Unless the items that belonged to their dad were also suffering from being overheated, there was something up. I guess looking back, I should have just asked

 59

him to leave since it was clear he was not going to think about the well-being of the kids.

My driver, at the time on this course of action, was that the kids should be allowed to finish the school year without having to go to school with a heavy cloud over their heads. I knew how this was hitting me, even though I was trying to hide it from the kids and others. I did not feel it was fair for the kids to not be respected because adults couldn't be adults. While yes, that dark cloud would still be there when they found out, and the summer was a certain level of hell, to move them forward as if *they would get over it* was not the type of parent I wanted to be. I am a strong woman and was able to cry in the corner by myself, wipe my tears, call a friend, cry, and scream, but I made sure that was when they were in bed. I navigated that month with every ounce of strength I had.

The next course of action, with his agreement, was that we would be very nice around each other. I was cordial with their father and even had to hug him occasionally to appease the kids who could tell that something was wrong with their parents. It wasn't fair, but I genuinely feel that when you have kids, you must be adult enough to do things the right way.

I gave my ex so many options to ensure, he was sure. I asked him if he wanted to go stay with his family in another province for a few months to think about things. He said no. I asked him if he wanted to stay with a friend for three months to think about things and I would watch the kids. He said no. The list goes on. I knew he was sure but wanted to make sure because if there was a slight chance that he wanted to change his mind, he had that opportunity. Because once we told the kids there would be no turning back.

The next course of action was that I told him that when we told the kids, we would have family there so that the kids were told in an environment of love and not abandonment.

For the fourth course of action, I told the teachers what was going on because I knew one of my sons was struggling at school, and while he was not aware yet, the signs were there that he knew something was happening. I asked them to give the kids extra love and empathy. They, as per usual, were amazing and stepped up to the plate on that one.

For the fifth course of action, I delegated him to find a therapist for the kids. I was in no shape to give energy to that, so I needed him to. He agreed and found one.

The next course of action was to implement some sort of routine for me. I leaned on my support system, which was my therapist, family, lots of friends, the gym, mindful behaviours, and much more. I also created a system for myself so I could get through each day, which I will tell you about a bit later. What I knew was that to get through this, I had to do things right and right away. I also knew, divinely knew, that the true healing process would not start until after the kids were told and when he had moved out. That was the moment I knew the true healing would begin.

One Saturday while I was home alone and the kids were at their dad's, I dedicated time to opening the book I was writing. I read it and read it some more. I realized that many revisions were needed, but I must say, it wasn't bad at all.

At the beginning of this book, I explain that it was a labour of love that was collecting dust on the shelf. However, this book was my template for true healing. Navigating pain, which I can only compare to the death of a loved one, was not easy. As it turned out, I had literally already written the book on that, I just needed to gain some maturity and make some revisions. Rereading, revising, and healing, I realized I was focused on three key areas to healing. Mind, body, and soul. All the items to help me heal and that will help you do the same, were under these categories. I've tried every trick in here, some were short and impactful, and others have served me for a long time. Either way, all of it works. Let's dive in!

EXERCISE:
WRITE A COMPASSION LETTER

Many years ago, I met an amazing woman who was a grief coach. She told me about her journey to this place and was passionate about supporting others through grief. I was fascinated by her because not only was this the first time I heard about this, but I became intrigued to listen to her insights about loss and grief. She told me about an exercise she typically gives to her clients, and I thought it was fantastic: write an empathy letter to yourself. These days, I lean towards the word compassion, so in this re-telling, I have chosen to call it a Compassion Letter.

1. Pull out paper and pen.
2. Grab some tissues because you will likely cry. (It's a good thing!)
3. Write the date at the top of the page.
4. Then address yourself, "Dear..."
5. Start by writing as small talk with yourself to break the ice.
   a. "Wow, it has been a dynamic year..."
   b. "I am so proud of how far you've come..."
6. Dive into the purpose of the letter.
   a. "While you have done so well, I think it is time to write a letter to reflect and show compassion to yourself..."
   b. "I am so proud of you however, you have to write this letter to ensure you are letting go, rising, and moving on..."

7. Then dive into the story.
    a. Reflect on what happened.
    b. Acknowledge how it hurt you.
    c. Acknowledge your feelings of anger that surface.
8. Then dive into compassion and forgiveness.
    a. Write about how you see how much this has hurt you, and how much it has changed you.
    b. Write down how important it is to be kind to yourself and write down ways you have been or plan to be kind to yourself.
    c. Write how this letter is an expression of self-compassion and how it is a contributor to your healing.
    d. Don't forget to forgive yourself and others that hurt you.
9. Write whatever you feel you need to get off your chest.
    a. Forgiveness (the person you broke up with, the friends and family that didn't show up the way you needed, the lack of compassion from others).
    b. Release of anger.
10. Then close it out with love, forgiveness, and a commitment to be strong.
    a. "Love you always..."
    b. "Stay strong and fierce..."

Exploring Gratitude

The state of being grateful.
Synonyms – appreciation, gratefulness,
and thankfulness

— Webster's Dictionary

I chose not to be a stay-at-home mom, although the conversation about being just that did come up. Probably more than once. While I love my kids, I feel that my childhood of extreme poverty contributed to my decision. I wanted to give my kids stability. I did not want them to live in fear like I always did. By the time I was 17 years old, I had moved 17 times and it was horrible. This was back in the late 80s and early 90s. Most of the time my friends didn't know where to find me.

Once I became an adult, I was pretty much convinced that it was exceedingly difficult to keep a consistent roof over your head, especially if you were a single parent. And here I was in a two-income relationship. The life we were living was amazingly comfortable to me. I was exhausted from being a working parent, but it felt amazing to not only keep the roof over our heads, but we could also go on vacation. I didn't want to mess with our finances. In addition, I am very career-minded. After all, I do have years of being a career coach on my resume. I also loved bringing in my own money. I never knew how the "it's our money" thing worked. I never had that stable home. I didn't know how people had the conversation about what the money looked like when there was a stay-at-home mom. Did I have to ask for money? What was I allowed to know about our finances? Those thoughts never sat right with me. Too much is unknown, and I knew that money management was not a strength in our house.

About five months before the divorce, my husband and I mutually decided that I would quit my job. I would take a part-time contract which would allow me to figure out my next career move and allow me to reduce the stress in my life which was driven by two things: my workplace and my marriage. I received the contract from someone in my network. They knew of my work and thought I would be a good fit. The timing was right, so I jumped on it. The contract would be half the money and no benefits; however, we still had his good benefits.

A few months later, he told me he wanted a divorce. Overnight, I was going to have to take on double the bills while making half the money. I was disappointed and furious at first. Here was someone who was crucial in this decision and yet it was clear that he had been looking to leave for a while. It felt like an attempt to disable me, and then crush me. Yet, initially, I felt fine.

First, in the career area, I rarely had any challenges. I was very mindful of my career and managed it relatively well. Second, I had skills that were unique enough to lead to new opportunities. Third, I had an amazing network of people who would have my back and be there for me (which they were). A fourth point reassured me as well—I have a strong faith and I knew that I would receive a great opportunity to replace the losses I was currently experiencing. And finally, I had not been out of work for longer than one month from the time I was 17 years old.

I started an overly aggressive job search which was hard as I was healing from this recent, tragic change in my life as well as that of my children. It was hard as hell. But I had a good group of supportive people. One of my besties was on the phone with me two to three times a week so we could discuss my applications and status. She reviewed all my applications to ensure I would send out strong, grammatically sound resumes. She had my back. Not to mention the people who had conversations with me, kept their ears to the ground for me and helped me keep my spirits up. It paid off—in less than six weeks I was able to secure a role. This ended up being a five-month contract with no benefits, but I was never scared of that. I knew if I worked hard, I could probably get it extended or become an employee. At the very least, I could pay my bills. First up, my hot water tank failed about three weeks into my new employment, so it was great to have the income to cover that.

What does this have to do with gratitude? I share this story not to focus on the down moments, but on the positives. I was able to be grateful for what I had which allowed me to get through the many significant challenges I was facing after divorce. Earning money is a huge one, people in my court to help me, security in how I had managed my career—all of which allowed me to rebound well and find work. Knowing that I had a strong faith which was essential to me getting out of bed and trudging through the thick and messy mud of a job search was a gift unlike any other. The list goes on. The point is that gratitude, and practising it, helps you to focus on what you appreciate versus what you want or expect. I was mindful of the things that were going well versus what was not. Even when I did feel sorry for myself, or frustrated, or deflated, or wanted to give up, I was able to remind myself that I had things to be grateful for. In addition to what I listed above, I was also grateful for my kids, the roof that was still over my head when so much else was taken away, a working car, good friends, a great relationship with my dad, and more.

Gratitude has been discussed by every successful person. No matter what, they will discuss gratitude for something and ensure they keep their head in the gratitude game. If you google your favourite celebrity—Oprah, J-Lo, Tony Robbins, Deepak Chopra, Beyoncé—and "gratitude quotes," you will find one of them quoting something on gratitude and the power of this tool to elevate your life. Oprah has a gratitude journal that she has sold for years. Focusing on facts, positive psychology has found neurological reasons for why people will benefit from the practice of expressing gratitude (positivepsychology.com). They note that it can enhance your well-being, deepen relationships, improve optimism, and increase happiness.

EXERCISE

1. Grab a few pieces of paper or cue cards. If you are using paper, make 31 cue card-sized pieces from it.
2. Write on one card or piece of paper, "30 things I am grateful for."
3. On each card, write one thing you are grateful for. This may seem hard, especially if you are not happy, so please use whatever resources you need to find things that resonate with you, such as Internet research, or look at your surroundings, pictures, etc.
4. Once you are done, fold each one and put them in a vase or jar.
5. Put that vase or jar in a place you visit often in your house.
6. Every morning or evening, pull one of them out and read it. Do this for 30 days and then start over again.
7. Add to the jar if you start to think of more things that you are grateful for over the month.

You want to heal. This is one of the reasons you are reading this book. Gratitude is an essential component of healing for several of the reasons listed above.

Getting Out of Your Comfort Zone

For years I wanted to go to Japan. I was always fascinated by it after learning about World War II. Not because of the war itself, but how the Japanese culture essentially pivoted into one of peace and love. I also love the seasons when they change. Specifically, spring and fall. Now, I live in a country where when the seasons change it is clear, and I get a great fall experience. But those cherry blossom trees you see in pictures of Japan seem like something out of a movie. In addition, SUSHI! I love some sushi. My bucket list is short, but Japan is at the top of that list. More than once over the last couple of years, I've said I would go, and I didn't. Over the past ten years, I've had the money, but I didn't go. I think it was a genuine fear of the unknown. There are quite a few people in my friends and family circle who knew this was my one place. And one day, in June 2020 (yes, COVID-19 season) my now ex-stepsister-in-law (if that is not a thing, we prefer not to change a title we love) sent me a text.

Her: Flights to Japan next April are only $515. (Multiple wide eye emojis.)
Me: Can I do that trip by myself?
Me: I feel like I should do that by myself.

Her: I feel like you should do it by yourself. (Smiley emoji with hearts around it.)

Her: I found the flights on Air Canada! I look every once in a while, for you.

Her: Cherry blossoms are in April too, I think!

On a side note, that is what real listeners do. They hear something, see an opportunity, and let you know.

Me: Hilarious, I have an Air Canada voucher for $550. How do I buy this?

Keep in mind that I rarely book a trip and was instantly so nervous that I did not think about how easy it might be. I sent her an affectionate emoji and said, "I will do it. Nervously, but I will. Wish me luck and thanks a million for thinking of me."

This text followed with a Love Yah Gif with Rachel McAdams in *Mean Girls*.

"Good luck (♥ ♥ ♥), love you!" she said.

She sent me the note on June 29th. I booked the trip on July 1st. It took me that long and a social distance wine night with friends to muster up the courage to book it. I let her know it was booked and asked for her prayers. She in turn sent a series of excited texts ending with a pregnancy picture update. She's a millennial; travelling is in their DNA. She was over it. Do you know what was the best part? I barely worried about anything for two days. Didn't contemplate when I should date according to my boredom and loneliness. Didn't think about anything, but this trip and if I should go. If this could take my mind off the mountain of stresses I had at the time, wasn't it a good thing? I was so in the moment, but I was also shifting my focus from what was in front of me to a better, brighter future. Taking yourself out of your comfort zone will do that.

Have you ever learned how to cook a certain food? Take an online class or watch YouTube. For 20 minutes of prep time and 30 minutes of cooking, you will not think of your ex or your circumstances. Have you ever wanted to take a painting class? For 30 minutes your mind will be so focused on "tiny little accidents" (thanks, Bob Ross) that you will not remember the person who hurt you. It is only until we are in our automatic, repetitive state that we get into a rut and miss the person or feel sorry for ourselves. Take yourself out of your comfort zone!

EXERCISE

1. Make a list of ten things you have always wanted to do. If you are unsure, google a top 1,000 list of things people have always wanted to do. Some ideas:

   a. Do you drive to work? Take the bus. Nothing will take you out of your comfort zone like that. Do it for one week.

   b. Love social media? Go off it for a week. You will realize how bad the habit is and be thankful you did.

   c. I've always wanted to go to a gun range. Do it! I heard it is quite a rush.

   d. Ever wanted to play an instrument? Book a lesson. One lesson should not break the bank. You can find independent instructors online. You can rent equipment if you need to.

   e. How about an overseas vacation?

2. Now that you have your list, circle three things that are relatively accessible, affordable, and can be organized or completed within a week or two.

3. Next, book and schedule at least one.

4. Now circle one that would take a bit of time to do. For example, if you want to go to Europe, but cannot get on a plane today because of COVID-19 or finances, this would be one to circle.

5. Now put this one in your calendar for six months to a year from now.

6. Plan for how you can accomplish this.

   a. Ask a friend to help keep you accountable for saving money.
   b. Maybe take money out of savings to book the flight and secure it (treat yourself).
   c. Start reading blogs on how to travel through Europe the best way (and the economical way if you are on a tight budget).

7. Repeat when you have completed some of this goal.

If you don't believe it works, stop, and think. How much did you think about your problems while trying to plan, organize, and figure this stuff out? See, it works.

Starting a Self-Confidence Plan

My self-confidence was out the window. My 2019 was a trauma I hadn't recovered from. Being told that your husband wants to divorce you after ten years of marriage is hard on your self-esteem. One year later, the COVID-19 pandemic occurred, and all the isolation, home schooling, and working full-time was wearing me down. Halfway through the year, I had a week that topped it all off. In one week, I had gained a pound even though I had been working out, I had found out my car was going to cost $3,000 to fix, my air conditioner/furnace failed five days past the warranty which cost me $1,700 to fix, I flunked a paper I wrote and got horrible reviews from my professor which made me feel stupid, and one of the tires on my car was slowly leaking air.

I went for ice cream with a friend because she was worried about me. My best friend was worried about me. While we don't typically call each other often, my father had reached out as he was worried about me. And I received a random call from a friend I hadn't spoken to in months who said I was on her mind, and she too became very worried about me.

No matter what is said, you go to a place of unworthiness like no other. You could be the most attractive, smartest, fittest, or most loving person, and suddenly you don't feel like any of those things. Now, obviously, we should never let anyone have that much power over us. We have not necessarily given that much power, but we become hyper-aware of how we are already feeling. If you have been in a long-term relationship or are not paying that much attention to yourself, you have already been struggling with some sort of self-confidence issue. Most of us do. Self-confidence, self-esteem is something that must be taught to us by the time we are seven years old. If not, then we must mindfully practice this for an extended period. When we are "being one" with someone else, we lose a bit of our identity, and we risk merging our levels of self-esteem with the other person. Just because they may have come across as self-confident does not mean they ever were. You took on some of that. Now is the time to realize that you need to create a self-confidence plan to rebuild yourself.

EXERCISE

1. When you were feeling the best about yourself, what did you love? List all the items.
2. Why did you love each one of these? Was it because you worked hard for it? Was it because you felt attractive? Was it because it was an accomplishment?
3. On a scale of one to ten (ten being the most), how self-confident did you feel about each one of those items you listed?
4. Would you love to feel that again?
5. If yes, what could help you reconnect with that feeling?

    a. If you were happy, in shape, can you create a plan to get back in shape? Do you have benefits that will pay for your personal trainer? Have you found a great workout plan on YouTube? Can you get up 30 minutes earlier each day?

    b. Did you receive a degree that you worked hard for? Can you take a low-cost course online and work toward a certificate?

    c. Did you receive praise for your last piano recital? Can you start taking lessons and practice again? Can you sign yourself up to play somewhere in two to three months?

We can have many excuses, but when it comes to self-esteem there should be no excuse to work to regain those feelings about ourselves. This is a crucial item to help you get the life you want. Honestly, if by chance you are still hoping that life is with your ex, I can promise you that if you regain your self-esteem, they will be intrigued by you again. The problem is you more than likely won't be interested in them anymore.

Increasing Your Self-Awareness

Losing our self-identity is a trap we all fall into. Some of us fall harder than others. In long-term romantic relationships where we share our life with someone else, our identity can become the relationship, itself. Even when we lose a long-term friendship we can feel as though we're missing a piece of our identity with that loss. Identity is important to all of us. We love knowing that we have something we connect to. Identity, in my eyes, gives you self-awareness. Knowing all the things that make you, you—knowing who you are—gives you a foundation that is strong and rarely unwavering. People see that. They admire it. They want it. When you have self-awareness, you have probably become aware of this influence by increasing self-reflection.

What is your political stance? What are your core values? What is your favourite colour? What is your primary love language? What do you enjoy doing? What do you hate doing? Who do you feel the most connected to that you know or who you admire? The list goes on but knowing the answers to questions like these helps us to understand who we are and to see the foundations of our identities. Why is this important? Because if we do not know who we are, how can we possibly know what complements us? How can we know what brings us joy? How can we know what we don't enjoy? How can we invite someone into our lives to connect with us on a deeper level? What do we feel about someone, beyond looks and physical attraction? Who are you?

Identity Before Nuptials

In my 20s, I was a hard-working girl who had zero direction in life. I knew I wanted more than what my life to date, had given, but had zero clues about how to achieve it, and was not surrounded by people who could help me figure it out. In my early 20s, I remember sitting with a group of friends discussing things we wanted. One said they wanted to be married with three kids. Everyone in the group saw that in her and knew she would be a great mother. We all discussed what that would look like for her as we could all visualize it. Another friend said she wanted to travel the world. We could see that in her. She had always been fascinated by different cultures, foods, and diversity. It was clear. We chatted for a while about where we thought she would go and what that would look like.

One of my friends turned to me and asked, "What do you see yourself doing?" I said I wanted to write books, be a best-selling author and be a millionaire." The room fell silent. Then, a little bit of snickering began. One friend piped up and said, "You are waaaaay too honest to be a writer." Dream shut down. I understood. I grew up in the gutter and had already made it way further than expected. At the time, I was making $20/hr at a good stable company that was not going away anytime soon. Should I not just be grateful for where I was versus trying to achieve more? For me, that answer is no. Even if it hurts and I fail, often I still get up and try again. It's hard for me to watch so I am sure the audience of my life struggles with the suspense. I never really did well with complacency, and I also knew that if I did not get up and try again, I would be sitting there watching someone else try to achieve their goals and eventually win. In other words, the world around me would still be trying and winning.

By the time I was 25 years old, I was finishing up a big girl's degree in business while getting my braces removed and looking to start my life. At this point, I had my heart broken too many times to count but kept getting up, dusting my shoulders off, and trying something new. I was about to head out on a trip with a friend to celebrate my graduation. It was exciting because I was starting to feel that life was giving me what I had been working hard to achieve.

After my trip, I made a major career shift that almost broke me. I was in a 100 per cent commission role as a Recruiter in third-party recruitment. Yes, pretty much head-hunting. It was a tough gig, and I was barely breaking even, let alone making the money I thought I would. But I would not quit. I keep getting up and dusting my shoulders off with every fall.

Identity During Marriage

When I got married it was all rapid fire. I married someone I had known for years and felt relatively safe around. I felt life would be more stable. I was transparent about being ambitious and wanting to achieve goals and my husband was fine with it. I had several failures along the way—more than I would ever like to admit and count. But I loved that I had this beautiful family to come home to, they kept me grounded and stable. I was living a dream better than I could imagine.

We had a house, which was the place I'd lived the longest in my life. Both my sons were born and came home to this place, and I am still here 11 years later. That is a massive success on its own. There has always been food in the fridge. The lights are always on. The heating bill is always paid. Things that, at times, were luxuries for me while growing up were nothing but normal to my kids. I had always achieved so much that by those things alone, I was starting to like stability. I knew this was something I enjoyed. I still had my hard-working side, but the stability side did not need to take a healthy chunk of my mind and I liked it.

During my marriage, I was passionate about the family including giving my kids experiences I had growing up (the good ones, like big birthday parties and playdates). I felt I had someone I could communicate with, even though it was clear we did not always see eye to eye on things like finances. I had stable friends. I was still feeling strong, navigating life's challenges as they came—and wow, did they still show up! Marriage was another thing, for me, which made me even more interesting. I had an approach that I think others didn't see. While the marriage ended, I was clear about some of the things that were important to me. While I communicated them before marriage, they were non-negotiable for me now.

Identity After Breakup

The first day I truly felt it—that clear void of not being whole—was when I picked up this book again to, at the time, read it,

 82

and now I guess to rewrite it. I felt like half of me was gone. I had to investigate that feeling to see if it was normal and apparently, it is. When you get married or are in a long-term relationship, part of your identity disappears. It just goes out the window. You are merging two people; their core values, beliefs, likes, dislikes, and everything else to build one strong unit. I compare this to when two companies merge. In case you don't have a business background I will give you an example.

Say, if Coca-Cola and Pepsi were to merge to be one company. This will never happen, but it is the best example I can give because we all know these two pops exist whether we drink them or not. So, say they merge. Everyone on the Coca-Cola side understood, adopted, and built their identity around its core values, beliefs, missions, and everything the company stood for. Same on the Pepsi side. But now the two are coming together to create one company. They now need to decide what the main mission is, what the new core values are, and what everyone is going to believe. Eventually, this will be agreed upon, and it will usually happen after one side is oddly just a bit more influential than the other. You decide, in marriage, what vines you are going to die on; what battles you are going to fight. Both of you will be able to stay very aligned with the things you truly, fundamentally, believe in and value. But with the other stuff, someone gives and someone bends.

Now that you are single again, you must find what you truly value, what you believe, and all the rest. You had these things before, but they have evolved and changed due to marriage.

Personal Reflection

I was always known as a strong girl. The girl who took no bullshit. The girl who was tough as nails. Along with that, I received the negative side of it: the girl who should be feared. The girl who was a loose cannon. The girl who had a bad attitude. The evil girl.

When you are single in your 40s, your wants and needs are much clearer than in your 20s. When I was in my 20s, I looked forward to Monday nights as that would be the start of my bar circuit week. Mondays were also when I would typically get laid by my booty call. I would work hard then play hard at night. Unhealthy for sure, but basically, the same routine. I was lucky that all I liked was alcohol and dancing. Once I hit 25, the need for that life diminished quickly and was replaced by an intense need to be more responsible and a drive to give myself a life. I wanted nothing more than to make better money, be more successful, and level up. I was driven by goals and missions, not booty calls and liquor. In my early 20s, I wanted pizza after the nightclub. I wanted sex whenever I could get it, and I wanted the nightclub to be the place where I would drink my pain away. I wanted to travel wherever the few dollars in my bank accounts could take me. By my mid-20s there was an obvious shift. I wanted money, stability, love, and a future.

In my early 30s, I was a new mom, a new wife, a new homeowner, a new person. I wanted nothing more than to protect and secure this identity. These were things I never knew I wanted, but when they showed up, I was all about them. I was busting my ass to protect this identity and often burning myself out in the process. I was working, mothering, wife-ing, and side-hustling to hopefully get something to stick. Failure after failure, sleepless night after sleepless night, I continued to push and wanted to believe with every ounce of my being that the effort was going to probably give me the equity I needed to secure this life I loved.

Now in my early 40s, recently divorced, revisiting who I am, and liking the process of finding that identity, I realize what I want is still clear. I want health and wealth for my family, I want to be a great mother, I still want to be a great wife, but to someone who wants me to be my best self. I want to live to be a glam-mother and continue the raising of my kids until I move on to meet my maker. I want to be in shape, I want to have freedom, and I want peace. I want stability and know that at least for now I must build the foundation for it. I am paying attention to more important things, like how to make more or cut down on expenses and contribute more to my kids' education fund. The list goes on.

Wants and needs change over time. Who we are—who we truly are—might stay the same. This is clear when you do something like a Myers-Briggs assessment. It typically stays the same over time. For me, it is clear who I am every time I read a card given to me by a friend years ago, that says the same thing as someone new in my life would describe me as, today. That I am strong, ambitious, loyal, kind, bold, and brave. I am love, have integrity, am accountable, aware of others, and am a friend. This list goes on and if you ever met anyone who knows me, you will be hard-pressed to hear them say I am not very, very, very, self-aware. I am also aware that things will change. When I am in my late 40s, 50s, and 80s, I will have new wants and desires. I will also still be me.

EXERCISE

This is a long one, but it is important because to heal we need to find ourselves again and this exercise will help you put some of those identity pieces together. I encourage you to do it in bite-size pieces as you continue to read this book.

1. Complete at least two of the following assessments. They are free and can be easily found online.
   a. 16 Personalities – this is a free Myers-Briggs assessment.
   b. Enneagram – this is a great assessment, especially to know how you change or act when you are going into a relationship.
   c. Love Languages – while I highly recommend the book, you can complete a free assessment online.
2. Once you have completed at least two, please read them.
   a. Circle or highlight keywords that stand out to you. Passion, integrity, funny, etc. Find those words. Circle it only if you feel like it sounds like you.
3. Ask a couple of your friends if these words describe you. Get confirmation.
4. Save this work, because later in this book we will discuss dating (when you are ready) and this information will be helpful.

Understanding People

*"Now that the marriage is over, do you feel you
would have left him anyway?"*
asked someone, just weeks after the end of my marriage.

*"Wow, you really dodged a bullet not being
with him much longer,"*
said another while I was having a meltdown about finances.

"You know you are going to do much better than him,"
said another person.

I could list these types of statements all day long. They are, as
you can see, poorly thought out and mindless. Saying stuff
like this does not help the situation. It only makes a person feel
lower when they are already low. It's hard for us to have the
emotional intelligence we need to understand people and their
actions when we are in the basement of our lives. However, we
must. We need to understand them because if we don't, we will
probably end up resenting them when no one meant to hurt us.

After the divorce, I found that I was being overly sensitive
when I talked to people. I was feeling like some people were
curious about the divorce and others were concerned about

me. While they were well-meaning people (at least, most of them) I knew this was an area in which I struggled, and I only felt motivated to talk to those I knew for sure were concerned about me, my well-being, and my kids' well-being. I didn't want to talk to people who were asking insensitive questions, triggering my trauma. I had to be protective so that I could transition through my healing.

A friend randomly texted me to talk because it had been a while, but the entire message had everything to do with her, and she never once asked me how I was doing or why had I been so silent. I responded with the Coles Notes' version of my last year (divorce, career change, therapy, kids, abundance of expenses, lots of challenges). She responded by saying she was sad for me and that I should call her because she missed me. I didn't feel good about it. This friendship was struggling anyway, but I did not want to make rash decisions. I did know that at this time, I had zero desire to indulge in small talk and relive my last two years with her. I let her know I was in a challenging space and was focusing on healing. I let her know that it had nothing to do with her, but that I did not want to relive the last two years over the phone. For me, there was no trust or safety there and I think we needed to tap into how we felt and go from there.

I like to ask people, are you in your basement? Your basement is that bottom-dwelling, dark place where you are not at your best. Think about a basement. If it is unfinished, it is typically a dark, dingy place that is not the best place to be. I got this term from the Gallup Strengths 2.0 assessment. When you complete it, you get five core strengths that are unique to you. These represent you, predominantly in the workplace, and how you apply your talents at work. This is one of my favourite assessments and

I highly recommend it, however, it costs money. Strengths are assessed with a list of balcony and basement statements. What this means is how do your strengths show up when you are in good times (balcony) and challenging times (basement)? Right now, you may be in your basement and if you are still there, your struggle is real. It is hard when you are there, to find compassion for others when you are in desperate need of compassion yourself. At that point, you feel like you could use a full-day hug or an all-expenses-paid week-long shopping spree. The challenge is that the people around you, after a while, are over it. Their lives are progressing, just like yours did when someone else went through this. It's not that they don't want to help you, but they probably no longer think about it as much and are also not sure what more they can do. The fact is, when you're in this space, they don't share your trauma and/or pain. You are in their thoughts but not in their routine. Don't take that harshly. Your challenge is in their thoughts. Trust me, they are thinking about you, but you are not in their routine. It takes a long time to create a habit. That habit would include texting you every day.

This I found true after the divorce, when I was around friends I typically enjoyed being around. It felt like there was a very prevalent shift in this group's friendship with me. It was unbelievably awkward to be around two of them especially, so much so that I would just rather not. It was unbelievably sad since I greatly enjoyed all our get-togethers before, but now I no longer tried to get us together or made an effort to join them. The last two times I was around them I felt invisible.

On top of that, I felt that when I was acknowledged, it was with poorly filtered questions that made me super upset inside and I had to just swallow them to get through the night. They were mostly odd questions around my ex. Some remarks seemed super insensitive, and I was just too sensitive to manage them. This was not their fault. They were being them. I mean really, as a society, how much time do we invest in learning how we can navigate life's challenges with people? We may have good intentions, but we don't do it well. Understanding and being compassionate for others when we are not in a good place is almost an impossible task. We might be able to in the beginning, but not for long. The reason is that the world would stop running if everyone stopped their lives because other people are going through shit.

Everyone goes through challenges, right?! Yes, those challenges are relative, but when we go through them, we desire compassion. This is probably why support groups are great, however, they are few and far between for divorced people. The thing is, if you don't have the support you need, the average divorce takes two to three years to get over. Even if someone dives into a new relationship, they are not fully over the last one. While you have this need, it is harder to be around people once they are "over it." I think the reasons why are as follows:

1. You feel anger toward them that is more than likely linked to the anger you still haven't fully let go of.
2. The animosity and disappointment you feel when they seem insensitive means you are revisiting that/those stage(s) of grief.
3. All in all, the feelings are a link to the pain you are still working through, and the loss you are still working through.

In truth, they do not know how to help you. Even if they experienced the same thing at one point in their lives, they have

 90

moved on. They are also not looking to constantly revisit that trauma/pain to appease you. Honestly, why would you expect them to? The truth for you, on the flip side, is that compassion is what you need. You need a friend(s) who can be there for you who can see that you are going through something and can let you vent on a bad day. The unfortunate truth is that the friends who can or are willing, will not always be who you expect, and it will impact the friendship. Sometimes people cannot see through their discomfort to meet you where you are at, where you need them to be. Avoidance can be the only solution, as that is how it feels.

I remember one day my oldest son got mad at me. It was out of nowhere and he was ten years old at the time. He felt I was giving my younger son (then eight years old) more attention. My sons and I have an agreement that when things get too heated, we take a breather, calm down, and come back and have a private conversation. Once we were calm, we had one of these private conversations. I apologized to him for his feelings and let him know that they were valid. Yes, I talk to my kids this way—they will be adults one day. I explained, "Right now, as I am sure you can agree, your brother needs a little more attention and love as he is struggling with COVID-19, no activities, and his ADHD." He was also still struggling with the divorce, and a couple of months prior had described to me that he was having sudden moments where he could barely breathe. He described panic attacks. I knew he needed help and that I had to get him that support. Between work, working from home during COVID-19, remote learning for school, and finding virtual resources to help him, and being extra observant of stuff, I was giving that child more attention. My oldest, at one point in his life, received that level of attention which is why today he doesn't need as much. I did not elaborate further, but simply stated, "He needs more attention right now, I am sure you agree." He did agree. He hugged me and then he apologized for getting mad at me. I told him there was no need and I was happy that he told me how he felt. I reminded him to tell me about these feelings before he became angry. He agreed. This was a conversation between a 42-year-old woman and a ten-year-old boy.

I used that scenario as an example because this can happen—we can have clear communication, understand what is going on from both points of view, meet each other where we are at, and let each other know what we can do moving forward. Often, we don't do this. I am not sure why. It typically gets to the point where the friendship just fades away or it returns to where it was, and someone brings up something from the past that sets everyone back.

The thing is, you are reading this, and your friends are not. You are the one looking for solutions to navigate this pain you're facing, or you would not be reading the books that help you. So, all I can do is give you tools and things to think about to equip yourself as you go through these challenging times. Unfortunately, someone must make a move, someone must meet someone where they are at, and sometimes that is going to be you.

EXERCISE

You only need to do this exercise if you feel like you have friendships that are in a rough place right now—relationships with people that have shifted, and you know that the tension has been elevated because of how you feel. Complete this exercise if you want to think through the relationship and determine where it may be in the future.

1. Ask yourself, how valuable is this relationship to you?

2. Think about the history of your relationship. Have you typically been there for each other?

3. What do they have going on right now? Create some awareness that there may be struggles in their world.

4. Do they typically act like this with friends when they are going through stuff? If the answer is yes, I am sure you know you don't have to continue the friendship. There is a pattern to notice here. You may just need to compartmentalize this friend and reset your brain to expect how they will show up in the future.

5. Do you feel comfortable having this conversation with them? If not now, in the future?

This exercise was important for me to do after the divorce. The shifts in many friendships were real. Why? Some of the friendships started after marriage. Some of them were because families got together with the kids. Some of them were because they were brought into the marriage. Once I completed this exercise, I was able to set my expectations and my head straight about the relationships I was concerning myself about. It was clear that with some, I should have never expected much from them. With others, it was quite a disappointment, and with others still, I was able to develop compassion for them because this was out of character.

Playing With Light in the Dark

Honestly, I would make this excuse too, but it was non-negotiable for me to make life happen again. I knew the stats. I knew that many times people take years to get through a divorce. I knew that all the stress could lead to serious depression if I did not care for myself. It was non-negotiable that I try anything and pray for divine energy in the process. I used every one of those mind, body, and soul tips and tricks.

The main regime I stick to is to pray, exercise, and journal or make affirmations, depending on the space I am in. These three powerful things have got me out of bed early, helped me start my day right, and moved me to a place where some people remarked that they would have never guessed what I was going through. Choose to apply ten per cent of this strategy. Most people just need to apply ten per cent and they are doing better than most. That does not mean you are at the same level of success as Oprah or Mel Robbins. Those ladies run at 110%. They have systems in place so that when shit hits the fan, they go through the process of that shit as quickly as possible. Believe me, they feel pain, I feel pain, but we are aware that pain is inevitable. Joy is inevitable as well, as is bliss, peace, etc. But they are not forever. If you measure your progress by reflecting on the season (spring, summer, fall, winter), you will notice that the changes are real. Spring brings blooms, like cherry and apple blossoms. Summer delivers bright sunny days, warm water, and barbecues. Fall ushers in golden leaves and chilly air. Winter brings beautiful snow and a season of jolliness. These seasons also present another perspective. Spring brings destructive storms. There are summer wildfires and heat stroke occurs; fall allergies and back-to-school bills; and seasonal depression in winter. The ladies I mentioned above prepare for the darker side of each season, and I try to prepare for that as well. It sucks but it is the truth. Where there is light there is darkness, but where there is darkness there is light. Prepare for both. Use tools, create systems, and you will get through each season, whatever side of it you are on, much better than most.

> *"In times of trouble, remember this: Who you think you are cannot handle this challenge, **but** who you really are can and will."*
>
> ~ UNKNOWN

The thing about life—whether we want to accept it or not—is that every day there is light (the sun rises) and every night there is darkness (the sun sets). When a kid goes to bed at night, that is when they will grow the most. Seventy-five per cent of their human growth hormone is activated during sleep. We can use darkness and light to represent daily life as well. We may hate the dark times, but most people who come out of that darkness have grown in some way—especially when they invested time into making sure their mind was strong, and that they were mindful of self-help, self-care, and self-love. They did not numb their pain with anything that did not serve them.

Here's what happens when you numb—you also numb the joy. You can't select the feelings you numb—you numb them all. So, if we can move through the dark times, the adversity, and the challenges, what is on the other side is joy. We grow from dark experiences, just as a child achieves most of their growth during the night when they are asleep. When we become adults, the best way for us to grow is through adversity. It's where we evolve, it is where we grow a new stem, and it's where we blossom. However, the process of going through this is so uncomfortable, we don't always find the silver linings in the challenges.

Believe You Are Worth It Because You Are

"What you believe you will achieve."

~ MARY KAY ASH

At one point I was dating an athlete, not a popular one, but one who was in televised sports. Due to the protection of the guilty, I cannot say who or what sport (trust me, he was no one famous and it was not the most global sport). It was not a fun ride. He was a liar, a cheat, and a sneaky jerk. Ours was a short-lived relationship that ended with no respectful conversation. It ended when I stopped putting in effort and him—being consistent—put in no effort.

It had been about two months since our last conversation when I suddenly received a call from him. He wanted to take me out for dinner and a movie, but just to talk. We had a nice dinner and went to the movie. I wish I could tell you what movie it was, but my anxiety was high because I felt that we were going to have an intense conversation. After the movie, we sat down and talked for a bit. He confessed that he was not exceptionally good to me, and he apologized. He said he regretted it and hoped I could give him another chance. Every

 98

woman who has been done wrong wants this moment. I didn't want it from this guy per se, but I know there is a guy or two I wish this happened with. I thanked him for those words and acknowledged how hard it would be to share something like that. In response to his request, I said, "I desire, demand, and deserve more than what you can give me." His face mirrored my feelings. Shock. I was shocked too. I just wasn't showing it. I could not believe that those words came out of my mouth. He didn't either. "Well, I am not going to give up. I will pursue you," he replied. He tried for two days and gave up. I was unphased.

I desire, demand, and deserve more in life. When I said those words, I truly believed them. To my core, I believed it. I knew that the person in front of me would never ensure that I had more. I am not talking about riches; I work hard for myself. I am talking about honesty, respect, accountability, great communication, intimacy over sex, and the many things that feed our souls in a relationship. I don't even know where that came from (demanding, desiring, deserving more). I had never heard that combination of words before. I never felt like I ever really advocated for myself in such a calm, matter-of-fact way before. I just know I honestly believed it.

There are times throughout life's journeys when I wish I had a genie in a bottle. One where Will Smith pops out and grants me three wishes. And there are times when I wish a falling star would shoot through the night sky and when I look up, I could have all my heart's desires. Mostly though, I pray. I pray hard on painful days and consistently on calmer days. Like a genie in a bottle or a falling star, we all believe the moment when we see it. I believe in prayer and the power of its divine energy to fill my soul as I navigate life's challenges. The point is, I believe. We all believe in something. We all inevitably believe in more. When we have a vessel, a genie in a bottle, falling star, or prayer, we tend to believe in more because we know in our hearts that it—He—can grant us all our heart's desires.

Your mindset is everything. It feeds your soul. Do not confuse believing that you should be with that person again, or that you should be a Lotto winner, with believing what you truly want and need. Foundationally, we know we should believe that we are worthy of everything the universe has for us. We believe we should have peace, respect, love, friendship, success, and the list go on. Those things do not align with potentially believing you should be with someone who doesn't want to be with you. Pay attention to what you believe you deserve.

Do you believe you deserve better than what has happened to you? Do you believe you are a good person? Do you believe you deserve amazing love? You and I both know you deserve so much. You deserve a person who cares about you the most and wants to give all you want, times ten. You deserve the amazing daydreams you have—the ones where you are holding hands, walking on a brick sidewalk in a nice part of town—the rom-com (romantic comedy) story where you bump into someone from junior high who was not a looker and has grown into his looks and is now looking at you, and so on. You deserve it. But you must truly believe it. You must believe you deserve it.

How can you believe it?

Here are three sound ways:

1. Start living your best life. Start taking control of the part you can, and the rest will follow. If you are sitting

on the couch all weekend long, you are not living your best life. If you feel there is no reason to get your hair done because you have not met anyone—that is not living your best life. If you wait to head out of town for a weekend getaway, you are not living your best life.

2. For 21 days, recite to yourself in the mirror, first thing in the morning, and at the end of the day, that you believe in yourself, and you know you deserve everything you dream of. Say it every day for the next 21 days. It will be hard at first because right now you don't believe it. But around day seven to ten, you will.

3. Read this list of affirmations every day:
   a. I am smart.
   b. I am wise.
   c. I am creative.
   d. I am intelligent.
   e. I am healthy.
   f. I am peaceful.
   g. I am happy that I am a great person.
   h. I am unique.
   i. I am deserving of great things.
   j. I am free.
   k. I am liberated.
   l. I am gifted.
   m. I am successful.
   n. I am brave.
   o. I am supported.
   p. I am loved.
   q. I am worth all my heart's desires.
   r. I am forgiveness.

Tell yourself there is no other option. The only option is to believe. And when that voice in your head tells you otherwise, you tell it to shut the f&*$ up. It does not pay the bills or maintain your relationships. That voice in your head is the negative friend you don't want to hang around with, but this one you can tell to go to hell, with little drama. You are entitled to this. Of all the things you are or are not entitled to, this one is clear. You deserve the very best. There is no question about that. Even serial killers who do deplorable stuff find love while locked in jail for the rest of their lives. If they can get that type of joy (and believe me, they feel entitled to it) then you deserve it. You believed one day you would drive a car and guess what, you probably do. Do you know how many people don't have a driver's license? Trust me, this is a flipping privilege. You believed that you could go buy groceries this week. Do you know how many people go to the food bank in North America? More than you can even fathom. So, believe you do and eventually that will be the truth you see in front of you.

Section 3:

Moving On

Moving Onward and Upward

It was late August 2019 when I picked up the original manuscript that I had written several years prior. If you were to ask me if this were the book I would finish and publish, I would have laughed. Even less than two years before, there was no reason or motivation to do so. But life happened and I was faced with the need for a manual—a manual I had already written and needed to revisit—a manual that was going to help me navigate the next days, months, and maybe even years depending on how the healing process went. It was one of the best gifts I gave my future self. The tools were written and now I share them with you.

I need to tell you, that moving forward, onward, and upward does not mean getting into a relationship as quickly as possible. If that happens and you are ready, great, but the intention with this book is to set the stage for you to develop a mindset that takes steps, even if they are baby ones, to move your life forward, to appreciate and master your experience(s) regardless, if you are single or not. Standing still in your pain, your hurt, your trauma, is relatively easy. I know this all too well and had to deal with it accordingly. But today, we rise. We rise faster to motivate ourselves to flow with the tide like the earth does around us. After a breakup, we feel like our world is standing still, and in essence that is probably the truth. One of my friends who suffered a tragic loss of a family member said it best, "It feels like the world around me is moving and flowing around me and I am paralyzed with grief and pain." I related because I was living with my grief at that moment, too.

Whether this is a fresh breakup or one that you have been healing from for a while, moving forward is a feeling which I would like everyone to experience. Some of us would love things to go back to the way they once were, and I wish you could get back to that moment where you felt love, support, and warmth from the person with whom you were in love. The reality is, that they no longer exist for you and even if they come back tomorrow, there is no "back to normal." It would not be the same. You will need to know what onward and upward can look like for you. How can you build that new level in your *Jumanji* (a movie that is about real-life people playing levels to exit the game)?

I want you to be able to take two steps forward and not eight steps back. The next few chapters contain exercises that allow you to connect with yourself and ignite a new abundance of energy for you. The following chapters have many tools and exercises so that when in doubt, you can revisit your wants and needs to help keep you in the game of moving forward. But before we start, I have a few questions for you to consider and write down:

1. Why do you want to move onward and upward? Here you may list things like your mental health, you deserve more, you want to live, etc.

2. What would onward and upward look like for you? Would it be having more self-esteem? A new hobby?

3. When you get there, what are you hoping is there with you? This could be either material or emotional. One of my goals was to not cry multiple times a day and be able to have a great big belly laugh that hurt.

What I ask of you is to be patient with yourself. Even—or maybe especially—on those days when you feel like you cannot handle the fact that things are moving along slower than you would like. Please, please, please be patient with the process and with yourself. For every win, I ask you to capture it and pat yourself on the back.

I remember my first belly laugh. I was watching Michel Che, from Saturday Night Live (SNL), do stand-up comedy on Netflix. I slept like a baby that night. I laughed so hard, then cried tears of joy. It took four months after the separation to experience a good belly laugh, and it took about three weeks after I picked up this book. I had forgotten about it and once I found it and started reading and rewriting, I started getting myself back together using these steps and this process. Take the time to pat yourself on the back for taking steps forward in the right direction and deciding to look at a future for yourself—one where you can truly start to feel like you are living life. That is my hope for you.

Figuring Out What You Want

Ihave an awesome career. I have had ups and downs, but overall, it has been fantastic. I have had dynamic, unconventional opportunities that have helped me to develop a strong work ethic and gain valuable skills, including an awesome understanding of people, and insights into diverse industries and experiences. This has worked for me. While most of my career has been in the service of others, there has been a focus on career and talent specializations, and specifically on coaching and acquisitions of talent. I want to focus on the coaching area for this example.

I was working on a contract, teaching a class of 15 professionals about workplace skills, to help them understand the soft skills needed to elevate their careers. Throughout the ten-week program, I would teach them a topic, and then we would end that topic with an exercise or project to help drive home the lesson. One exercise was on self-awareness and how it helps with career management. I believe that self-awareness is the foundational ability that allows you to understand others in the workplace and to manage the various dynamics that arise.

I started the exercise by letting the class know about the areas of life which should be as balanced as possible to help us live a relatively pleasant life. What is important to one person is not necessarily important to another. You may have abundance in one area and are severely lacking in another, which is what causes challenges. These lists typically range from eight to 12 items, depending on which source you refer to. For this course, I condensed the list into nine areas based on my interpretations of the information available.

- Finances (savings, investments, control, etc.)
- Relationships (love, romance, single life)
- Family and friends (social life, fun, community)
- Spirituality
- Career
- Health (nutrition, exercise)
- Education (continued learning, reading, courses)
- Recreation (hobbies, sports, travel)
- Community (charity, volunteering)

I presented these as crucial areas of life that we should always keep track of in our minds. The next step was for them to grade each area of their life. After that, I had them write about what was going well in each and what could be improved.

The purpose of this exercise is to know where you truly are, at this moment. People think that they know what would make them happy, and half the time it is not that at all. Would getting into another relationship right now make you happy? Or would it simply give you a temporary sense of relief from pain? We explored this in the class, as it ensures people understand where they are in this process. Then we would take that information and write a letter/declaration to ourselves. This will be your exercise for this chapter.

The goal is to become very aware of what you want, what you need, and to have increased self-awareness. Once we can see that, the important thing is to prioritize. What needs attention today and what needs attention a little later? Writing it in a letter to yourself, discussing what you need and want, allows you to clearly declare those things.

EXERCISE

1. Take a piece of paper and write down the nine areas of life.

2. For each one, grade it out of five (one being low, three the middle, and five being the highest).

3. Based on what you see, what areas need the most attention right now, and which ones are good as they are?

4. Take the one that needs the most attention, write it at the top of a new piece of paper, and write why you think this is an area that requires more support. As well, write about the impact this area is having on your life. Then add some solutions to help increase the score towards a five. Write down some possible ways to do this. For example, based on the theme of this book, relationships may be the most neglected right now. Is it romance? Is it companionship? Do you desire to be happy with being single? Who can help you to level up in this area?

5. Then write down the next area of life that is the most challenging for you and go through the above steps again. Continue to do this in the order of the most challenging areas to the areas that are doing well.

6. Once you have completed the above, it is time to put some of this into action with accountability.

   a. Grab a piece of paper and write a letter to yourself.

   b. Start by validating your current state and what you hope to improve.

   c. Reflect on the areas of life and discuss your awareness of how improving those challenging areas would benefit your life. Discuss what is going well and express how grateful you are for these areas. Discuss why and how those things are positively impacting you.

   d. Discuss what you might have to do to elevate the lower-scoring areas, and what you could do to maintain the areas in which you are doing well.

Reactivate Your Dreams

In 2004, I was in an intense relationship that ended almost as quickly as it started. It was one of those relationships in which it was easy to get distracted. People loved that we were together—they were all about our union. It brought people together for a short period. Then out of nowhere, it was done. Just didn't work. Maybe too fast, too soon, but it just did not work. I didn't over-analyze it, but I knew it couldn't work. We mutually cut ties and away we went.

While it was short, the relationship had a massive impact on me. I woke up the next day sobbing, very distraught by the breakup. I knew my feelings were valid, but I couldn't quite reconcile why I was feeling this way until about a week later. I knew that relationship was a welcome distraction from the many dreams that started to surface in my life; one of them was to go back to school and get a degree. This was super scary. I lived on my own, barely got by on my pay, did not have parents to lean on to top up my pay or pay for school, and there were zero savings to cover the costs. I wanted a degree though and it was devastating to me that to get it, I was going to have to take a route that was going to be extremely hard and exhausting. While I was in that relationship, I didn't think about it. I just enjoyed being with—and talking to—that person, and I was quickly forgetting about my desire for further education.

Once the relationship ended, those dreams resurfaced and the strongest one was to get a degree. I did not want student loans and I wasn't sure how I was going to make it happen, but because it was such an overwhelming push to get things done, I knew I had to find a way. I searched for a program that could accommodate my full-time work schedule. At that time, online schooling was not that popular in my city, let alone in the country. I investigated financing and was registered to start the following semester. It was a lot to think about and I didn't receive much support. In fact, many thought I was making a rash decision, and others just thought I would fail.

The journey was tough. I burned myself out several times; had a couple of mini breakdowns along the way. I gained and lost weight. I fell in love and lost love. I had a car I loved, stop working, and had to buy a beater that left me afraid to drive. I was broke at times and sometimes unpleasant to be around. But I did it! I completed my degree and after graduation, I went on vacation to the Dominican Republic with a friend to celebrate. It was my first trip out of the country since I was 13 years old. Travel, by the way, was another item on that list of dreams.

Many times, we lose ourselves in a relationship. I don't know if that is necessarily bad, but when a dream dies because of the relationship, that is the tragedy. Why do they have to die? Why can't we make sure we are with a partner that will support our dreams? Well, I have a theory. We just see something more obtainable when we are with this person. We also see something more relatable to others. We see a marriage, kids, house, car, and vacations. We see others living that life and we know that is obtainable. But for some dreams—like writing the book that has been weighing on our hearts—we haven't seen anyone else achieving them, so they seem unattainable. I know more doctors than I know authors and I am in my early 40s with a vast network of friends.

Our dreams may also feel risky. We may fear they will cost us money, relationships, everything that we currently enjoy. And we are not always willing to take those risks. While we hear these amazing stories of rags-to-riches success, it is also not uncommon to hear how people sacrifice, lose everything, and then rise again. I do not even like roller coaster rides and yet, it is the journey we should be focusing on, not just what could be on the other side of that dream. Below is an example.

From the time she was young, a woman dreamed that she was going to marry a tall, rich, handsome man. She was 25 years old when that dream came true. She had all she wanted. She didn't think that this dream had risks. One day, her husband came home and said he was terminally ill. There was nothing in her dream about this situation. She wanted that dream and because it was commonplace, she didn't consider the risks. This is not me telling you to live in fear, but quite the contrary—I would love everyone to get married. You learn about abundance for yourself. If you can, do it. The dreams you once put in a box in your mental storage space have the same risks, we can just see those risks more than in other, more common scenarios. Or maybe we don't see the risks and don't like the idea that following a dream off a beaten path may bring isolation.

The point is that your dreams are yours and they were given to you for a reason. They are desires and wishes that you once wanted. They are motivation in a storage box in your mind—something that can help you look forward and move forward. The journalling exercise in this book can jumpstart your motivation to finally write that book or follow that passion. To get moving, you may be encouraged to become a part-time fitness instructor and train for a race. You want to revisit those dreams and activate at least one, without focusing on anything except the journey towards the dream. Remember, this book is technically over 13 years old. It would never have seen the light of day without my steps to revisit my dreams. I happened to have written a book that is good but needed some modern tweaking.

EXERCISE

What are your dreams? Let us dive in and figure out those dreams and ways in which to activate them.

1. Using the Notes app on your phone or a piece of paper, jot down five to ten dreams you may have had over the years. Did you dream of kayaking in a picturesque lake? Did you dream of becoming an avid hiker? Have you dreamed of seeing both oceans? Have you always wanted to learn how to cook more than boiled hotdogs? Maybe you want to open an ice cream shop. Whatever your dreams are, write them down.

2. Next, look at that list and circle the top three that call to you. These are the ones you have told others about over the years. The ones that you say, "If I had the time, I would do (x)."

3. Research the "how-to" for each one. Learn about how to start the hobby or where you can get lessons and capture the how-to for each. Write at least a half page of notes on each one. Find out how much equipment you may need and cost it out.

4. See which one is within your means right now. If you are on a tight budget and one of them will only cost $20 to start, I suggest starting with that one. Maybe one of your dreams was to develop your painting skills. Paint nights are incredibly fun and low-cost. This is a great way to start.

 117

5. Plan for the other two to three. Saving money for them should be part of your plan. Keep in mind that everything will require some sort of resource. If you are looking to start skiing and won't be able to save much money, think about renting equipment and asking a friend to teach you the basics. If you want to see an ocean, but cannot afford a plane ticket, check out bus deals or ask a friend to do a road trip with you one year, and the next year ask another friend to get to the other coast. Include a timeline for each and get it in your calendar.

6. Create a vision board for these dreams. Make sure that they are visible somewhere for you to see often. This is important because what you can see, you believe.

7. Be accountable and enjoy the process. Promise yourself you will try, and you will enjoy the process while you're at it. I can't say you will write the next best-selling book or that you will be able to become a lawyer, but what you could learn on the journey will not only positively impact you, but those around you. Knowledge is power and it helps to broaden our minds.

One year, I did this exact exercise. I had ten items on that list and by the end of the year, I had accomplished/completed six out of ten. Did I fail? No, not at all. In fact, because I could see that I had achieved something substantial, I was so impressed with myself. Yes, I patted myself on the back for that. A year from now, you will be patting yourself on the back, too.

Get Moving

My divorce was decided on a Friday. On the following Monday, I was back at the gym. I remember I cried on the drive there, and I cried on the drive home. When I walked inside, I had my hood up and my eyes on the ground. I ran on the treadmill, rowed on the rowing machine, and lifted weights, with a few quick runs into the change room to cry quietly in a bathroom stall. I mean, how does one get back to the gym that quickly?

Looking at the stages of grief, it seems like I was in denial, and I was, as I later learned. Serious denial. My mind knew, but my body didn't. I just did what I knew to do when I was frustrated. Go work out. I had motivators too. The first was that, at the time, my kids didn't know. It was crucial for me to let them end the school year before finding out. Why? I would hope that is obvious, but in case it's not, who wants to find out their parents are divorcing on a Saturday, then go to school, likely breaking out in tears daily for the rest of the school year? I knew my kids loved my marriage and I knew it would hit them hard. While I was struggling with an intense amount of pain, I had to dig deep and manage it for their sake. Many say their kids are their priority, but I struggle with that. There is rarely a child who does not want to believe their parents will stay together forever unless the relationship is clearly toxic.

And even then, some kids just do not get why their parents couldn't find help to fix their problems. Then parents wonder why their kids grow up repeating those exact cycles. There is no role model for action. Get help for challenges. Try harder. If it doesn't work, then separate in a way that the kids remain the top priority. For me, I was adamant that they be put first. While my kids knew something was up, they were not fully aware and that was important. Their teachers saw them behave the same way, and I knew this because I asked them. I let them in on the situation because I wanted to request that if their behaviour changed, that they be a little more compassionate with them. As I mentioned before, they are weather babies—they know when a storm is coming.

Another reason I was in that gym on Monday morning was that I needed a booster—I had to manage myself as best as I could. Exercise has been proven to have an abundance of benefits. A few of the most recent pitches I have seen over the years that build the case for exercise are:

- Decreases depression.
- Weight loss.
- Lowers cholesterol.
- Increases self-confidence.
- Increases happiness.
- Reduces stress.
- Increases focus.
- Increases energy.
- Improves sleep quality.

Divine strength guided me to that gym every week, and over time it became a sacred space where I could redirect my pain from my heart and mind into muscle and ligament. For brief, yet intense moments, I forgot my worries. The earlier my morning workout, the better my day would be.

Getting moving is going to be challenging at times, but you can do it. On easy days, I roll out of bed at 5:00 am and get moving. On challenging days, in the words of Evangelist Joyce Rodgers, "I just need to reach up into the heavenly and grab big!" In other words, I must tap into divine strength.

Truthfully, I cannot stand working out—I do it for the aftereffects. Getting up at five in the morning, packing a gym bag, and hopping in the car takes a lot out of me, and I haven't even begun the workout yet. I still need to change my clothes, put on my running shoes, come out of the change room, and choose a piece of equipment. After any workout, I feel as though I have accomplished one of the greatest things on earth and that the world is now my oyster. It's kind of like that feeling of falling in love, except this time it is with yourself. Finding momentum is tough, but I quickly gain confidence, lose weight, tone up, and quiet the negative voices.

Not everyone's default setting is to hit the gym the moment after something like this happens, or it might not be to hit the gym at all. You might enjoy other ways of getting active. Maybe you like golf, hiking, or riding a bike. Whatever it may be, the point is to get moving and for you to start small and build upon it. I will give you tips to start small. The key here is to get moving and to move for at least ten minutes to start—less than one per cent of your day. An hour is less than five per cent. Did you know that? That includes sleeping hours, so if we focus on a typical day, minus six to eight hours of sleep, one hour out of a 16 or 18-hour day, is roughly five to six per cent. When you see it that way, you can give focus on moving for ten minutes. Psychologists have proven ten minutes of brisk movement can increase your energy levels significantly (Psychology Today). Do a search on YouTube for ten-minute workouts and you'll find an abundance of amazing videos—from sit-ups to basketball, to hitting the stairs. Set your timer and see how fast ten minutes go by. You will feel more energetic, and you will want that feeling again. You won't get in shape in ten minutes a day, but you're planting the seed for better physical health, a better mood, and better mental health. It's a start. You are important and this is making time for you.

Any workout plan needs music. Music is a form of vibration, and it helps align us with that good-feeling place. Thankfully, it has never been more accessible. If you have a smartphone, you've got music. You can get earbuds for free with your phone or cheap at the Dollar Store. I highly recommend you create a playlist as soon as possible. You need music that will get you going. I do not know how people can work out without gym tunes. Most gyms play music, but having your own playlist with *your* music that goes with *your* rhythm, is better. These will be songs that get you into a happy place. It can be anything from 90s RnB to 80s classics, to anything by Eminem, or hard rock. Check out carlilance.com for some great sample playlists.

When I work out, I am repeatedly startled off my treadmill because I am in such a trance with my signature Dr. Dre song, that I cannot even sense when someone is trying to get my attention. When I am at a crowded gym, I barely notice anyone because my theme music is playing, and I am in my own world. I need music. I am sure most moms and grandmas would not want to hear my music, and it would make a priest faint, but it works for me. This intense and over the edge music helps me to relieve my aggression. My playlist includes more common artists, such as Eminem (rap), Metallica (rock), Bounty Killa (Reggae), Skepta (rap), White Stripes (rock), Pussycat Dolls (pop), Onyx (rap), and Fall Out Boy (rock), but is focused on some of the harder music produced by these artists. They get me pumped.

To get you jump-started into moving, here is a list of tips. They are not focused on just going to the gym since I know that is not for everyone. This is a list of diverse tips for almost any scenario, and it will help minimize excuses.

TIPS:

1. Get an accountability buddy—someone you can report your progress to and from whom you can get support.
2. Make that playlist! You will be glad you did.
3. Choose something to focus on and commit to for 21 days. This could be going for a ten-minute walk every day, hopping on your bike for 15-20 minutes a day, a ten-minute yoga session on YouTube every day, walking up and down the stairs in your home for ten to 20 times, or a squat challenge you can find on Pinterest.

When we are not at our best, motivation to do anything is tough. All we want to do is eat chips and binge-watch TV. These small little exercises, implemented daily, will help boost your mood and help you feel better about yourself. They are small wins with massive rewards.

Boosting Your Social Life

One day, I was super excited for an after-work patio hour with friends. I wore my power red dress and confidently strutted my stuff along Stephen Avenue—a quaint, art installation-laden street in my city. We were heading to the Cactus Club restaurant, and I was excited to catch up with two of my friends. What made this even more awesome was that the two friends I was meeting had never met before. And one of my friends was bringing a friend. As you know, this could either work well or fail miserably. Lucky for us, it worked very well. You would never guess some of us had just met each other for the first time. The conversation was so fantastic it withstood a brief rainstorm that poured over the umbrellas that were propped up promptly by the amazing workers at this restaurant. We talked about online dating, divorce, hot topics in the news, about the future (of course this was months before COVID-19), and more. It was one of those after-work cocktail sessions that could have gone on until the restaurant closed, but we had other responsibilities.

Even with all these positive reasons, they were not what made this patio banter great. What made a simple cocktail hour so awesome, was progress. This was only three months after the divorce announcement. I looked good, felt good, and was all about a great conversation. I was open about the divorce without having meltdowns (not that there's anything wrong with that). One friend said, "You certainly don't look like someone going through a divorce," and I said, "Thank you."

When I experienced heartache in my 20s, I went into a cocoon. I went off the radar and only came out for work and food. That was it. Then it was work, food, and the gym to burn off the pounds I gained from my hibernation. It was not healthy and the only thing I lost was time, and eventually weight I could have avoided gaining in the first place. That process/system did not work. This time things had to be different.

When I determined the divorce was a go, I instantly turned to people. I went to my dad's that night and in a state of brokenness, I told him and my stepmom. I felt the need to face the music that this was for real and was not going to change. I was embarrassed, crushed, and felt like a failure. I also knew, maybe because I am wiser in my 40s, that isolation is not a good thing. It's unhealthy and scary. The National Institute for Aging states: "Research has linked social isolation and loneliness to higher risks for a variety of physical and mental conditions: high blood pressure, heart disease, obesity, a weakened immune system, anxiety, depression, cognitive decline, Alzheimer's disease, and even death." It is not good. When you isolate yourself, you are alone with your thoughts and your pain. In this area, the only solution is to take some initiative, rip off the damn Band-Aid, and get out.

One thing most people will tell you when they are grieving a loss is that the world around them continues to move while theirs stands still. Getting reacquainted with the world allows you to start moving with the tide again. It may be slow at first

and feel awkward, but after one or two good nights out, or afternoon patio lunches, or a brunch with a friend, or even meeting new people at a paint night, you will start to see your life in motion again.

Social isolation makes you miss the action around you. You miss the updates on people. Yes, we have social media, but it is noisy, and you end up missing key things in your friends' lives if you go into isolation. You alienate yourself from everyone. Dr. Eric Jenson, who holds a Ph.D. in Human Development, said, "We are social beings, and our brains grow in a social environment." He is an educator who taught other educators how to teach the diverse brains that would be in their classroom. He knows the brain. But what this means is that being around people laughing, talking, and hugging allows our brains to get back into the game. Get back into the swing of things: find a hobby, plan a getaway, or join an adult recreation team. This does not necessarily mean you have to beg your friends to hang out but having a coffee with one at a time won't hurt. Make new friends if you like. Pick up a hobby that provides a great place to dip your toes in the social waters. Fill your calendar with activities. They could include a book you want to read, a fun night out with your friends, taking a course, learning to use a paddleboard, or painting your home. Live your life because we are not guaranteed a tomorrow. People want to see you happy. Yes, that could be so that they feel more comfortable around you, but it is mainly because people genuinely love joy. Even if they are miserable. And they want you to be happy because it is contagious. As tough as it may be, fake it a little, at least until you realize this is what you want as well.

Finding Your Formula
for Rapid Healing

This was it—the last birthday party I would throw for my boys before they would start to live in two worlds. It was the annual birthday party for my two sons. I have always thrown their parties on the same day because their birthdays are 17 days apart. When you pool the money for one birthday, and most of their friends have brothers or siblings who would be attending anyway, it was best to throw one big party. Maybe that was just my rationale to justify throwing a party. This year, it was thrown together with a last-minute booking of a gaming truck (a truck that is filled with video games for kids to play), and with a little support from some friends to get things going, and some support from their dad, I was able to get this party started. It wasn't easy. I was hustling to get decorations, send invites, ensure the cakes were made, remember who to invite, and book the truck. All this, just days before they would be told that their parents were going their separate ways. It was much-needed joy for both boys.

It was also, for some strange reason, the last night that their father lived in the house. He technically finished moving out before the party was even finished. It was mind-boggling and came with many attacks on me about how I would not tell him off. I was not going to be the person to correct a moral compass.

It wasn't my responsibility. Besides telling him off would mean the boys would see what they had not seen from me through the entire process—anger.

During the party, one of the parents who stuck around said, "So, I was shocked when I heard the news. I still am shocked." I just looked up and nodded. They went on to say, "But you look like you are handling it well. You look great for someone going through a divorce."

Oddly enough, many people said that which is a strange thing to say, but I guess divorce has a look. The look is the difference in your stance. It is the difference in your speech. But the part that I see in anyone who grieves, is the absence of life in their eyes. It is like they are lacking in the vitamins and minerals of life. They are deficient. That is the look of it. The thing is, I did have that look when I could let my guard down and be me. My kids, well, that wasn't something they had to see in their mom. I responded, "If someone wants to go so badly, hurt the people they claim to love this badly, you have to let them go. Whatever they are going to is clearly what they need more." I went on to say, "As for my looks, my makeup is my suit of armour. I have been training for this battle since Grade Nine."

That normal look I donned, and which was unexpected for someone who is freshly divorced, was a look that came with many routines that I instantly adopted to help manage the day-to-day. At first, it was hard to get into the routine, but I saw no other option if I wanted to function. I had a massive mountain I was going to have to climb, soon. I had a mortgage I was going to have to take on myself, double the bills to maintain my home, and house maintenance to manage. I was also going to have to dive into a new job search just months before I had left a very lucrative job to "be less stressed at home." This was 2019 and the market was not so savoury. I was going to have to navigate an abundance of change.

People leave you for no reason when this happens. It was shocking to realize the number of them. I had to manage my emotions. Not just my emotions, but to be a solid shoulder, a listening ear, a source of comfort, a sounding board for my two sons whose world was in a tidal wave of change. The list of the things that I was going to have to battle and navigate was long, but the main reason why I was suited and booted was that I got into rapid healing mode.

The items I am about to divulge, helped me to get where I am less than two years later, with a great career in a great company, more money than I made in the job I walked away from, and amazing benefits. Those benefits include four weeks of vacation, accounting training, a wellness account, employer-paid benefits, and the ability to work from home when COVID-19 hit. I haven't been to the office since the first lockdown in March 2020.

I am in a place now where my kids are happy and feel heard and seen in this process (their words). I have the resources and the means to get them the support they need and want at any time. My mortgage is under my name, and my bills are more than just paid, they have credits on the accounts. I still have many of my friends and have grieved the relationships I have lost over the last year and a half. I am in a place where I see the sun in an open field, not just a small glimmer of light at the end of the tunnel. I am here, putting myself out there and exploring the world of dating, learning a lot about myself, including how brave I can be if I want to be. I have lost 15 lbs and have not looked this good since before the kids were born.

So how did I get here? What is my formula for rapid healing? Rapid healing really means rapid coping. There is no quick fix that will solve the problem. Anyone who sells you that is selling you a bill of goods that will probably put you in a bad position in life. My formula, with commitment, has all the proof backing up each item. Set a routine incorporating all these items into your daily schedule, and you will be in a place that is much better than where you are now (unless of course, you are perfectly fine and just want more tips and they are still great to practice).

First

You must believe in something and find a way to connect to it daily. In my case, that is my belief in God. Yup, the big kahuna. I am all about the Father, the Son, and the Holy Spirit. I am a Catholic Christian who loves Jesus but cusses a lot. The greatest thing about believing in God is that when I feel like there is no physical being around me that is supporting me, loving me, caring about me, or there for me, I believe that God is doing all those things and I turn to Him. When I am low, knowing that something is listening to me is great. We all want to be heard, right? There is community with God. You need to find a healthy community, but that goes with everything.

I mentioned God. For others, it could be Buddha. It could be the Universe. Think about what that is for you, connect to it as quickly as you can, and immediately start communicating all your pain, frustrations, wishes, hopes, and wants into that belief.

Second

Find an outlet and purge. For me, that was writing in a journal every morning. My minimum was three pages. I purged whatever came across my mind. At the time, it was a lot. When you are flooded with emotions and pain you have a lot to say. In ten months, I filled two to three full journals.

If writing is not your jam, you can do an exercise called "100 videos". You record yourself while purging on one topic. For you, it will be the feelings you are going through with this breakup, and perhaps, how you want to heal and move on with your life. You don't have to show these videos to anyone, but they are there for you to review later if you like. If the thought of being on camera makes you cringe, you can also use the voice recorder option on your phone. There is no excuse when you need to heal. You must do the work, so try something.

Third

Get active. You have no choice here. You must move your body in whichever way that may look for you. The scientific proof of this is irrefutable at this point, so make the moves. Whatever the movement is, you need to keep to a committed schedule of 30 minutes a day. If you cringe at that, I will let you know that this is less than eight per cent of the time in your day. You and I both know you recently committed that much time to social media or some trash TV show. Yes, it will be a change that will require you to adjust. That is usually why we don't do these things because change is hard, even if it is good for you. Take your pick, just commit and establish a routine.

These formulas must be activated to work. It is no different than starting a new diet or learning a new skill. At first, it may feel like work, I won't lie. As a result, it is important to remind yourself of your why. Post notes everywhere you can think of to remind yourself of your why. The notes could say:

1. Because it beats being miserable.
2. Because I deserve more.
3. Because this must have a better outcome.
4. Because I want to feel better.
5. Because I deserve some control.

The list goes on, but you get it. Post these on your computer, on your mirror in your washroom, on the wall beside your bed. Attach one to your remote control for your TV, and by your coffee maker—everywhere you can think of, so you are constantly reminded of your why.

My last pitch for this practice is that you will increase accountability to yourself. You will increase your self-awareness. You will help your mood and you will get back to a place where you are more neutral. I cannot say when it will happen, but you will know, I promise, that it has happened. For me, it was the day I could smile and laugh, when I had that deep belly laugh while I was out with friends. It was the first time that I laughed without fear, remorse attached to it, or without forcing it to happen. If you are divorced, they say it could take two to three years to heal from this. However, this practice will help you get to a place where you function and heal much faster. You want to get to a place where you feel like you are part of the world again. If you are already there, then great, but we can still incorporate practices that will help us to continue, on the path forward.

Managing Change After a Breakup - The Friendship Challenge

I couldn't put my finger on why, but I knew this feeling was challenging to manage. I was disconnecting quickly from a group of friends. When I saw a text or a thread, I instantly felt animosity and anger rise to the surface. I managed my feelings and was polite with my responses, but I was struggling. I hate when I can't put my finger on why I'm feeling a particular way and want to get to the bottom of the puzzle. I knew it was a me-problem. I knew it was my battle and I had to figure it out and address it promptly.

One day I was chatting with my bestie in Toronto explaining my struggle when I started crying and the flood gates opened. I felt this group of friends was being insensitive to me, that they weren't supportive as I navigated the divorce. It was awkward to be around them because up until this point, we had been four families spending time together, and now my family had changed significantly, and I was not feeling comfortable doing "family things" quite yet. My friend validated these feelings and told me that if this is how I felt, then I had a right to those feelings. She reminded me that I was the one healing. I didn't wish bad blood on them, I just felt that I couldn't accommodate them. They acted as though nothing had changed, but I had changed, and my family had too. There it was, I had identified the challenge and how it was impacting the dynamics with this group of friends. I continued to explore those feelings.

If this had been five days before the initial separation, I would have reasonable expectations of these friends. I knew that it would be the status quo. However, I had changed, and I required them to acknowledge, validate, and accept that change. Beyond that, I needed them to accommodate these changes somewhat, to adapt to our friendship.

I am now on a dynamic schedule, mandated by the courts. If I don't have my kids on a weekend, I cannot accommodate a group outing that day. If it is frustrating for my friends, I can't do anything about it. Nor should have I to.

Many changes occur after you have been in a relationship for a long time. When the relationship ends, so much of you changes. You must adjust to this new life. You must organize your bills, learn how to live on one income, manage the emotions of your children, change this, and change that. You are constantly running and addressing your emotions as they surface. They say the average divorce takes two to three years to get over, which means it could be a full two years before you start feeling more like yourself. I was out with friends one Saturday night, a year and a half after the separation, and told them that for the first time I felt, partially, like myself again. They confirmed that they felt they were seeing me again, too.

When you begin a relationship or are significantly into it, you may also change a lot. You may start to cancel plans and lose pieces of your identity, bit by bit. You start to settle down and get more comfortable with popcorn and wine nights versus Saturday club nights with girlfriends. You love having someone to snuggle with and enjoy doing a couple of things with other people—even meeting new people. You start to see what another side of life could look like, and you like it. You live it. Friendships fade and you make your peace with that. Add marriage and kids, and things change even more. You lose touch with people and with some, it's not a big deal—you can always pick up where you left off. Others will take it very personally and be frustrated with you. Once a relationship is over, and you are on the other side of the breakup, you recognize that only so many people remain with you. Some friends show up during this time in a big way and others do not—and they're not always the ones you would expect. Some may be curious, and some concerned. Some may share their stories about changes in their relationship, and others might look at you as if your breakup could be contagious. Some will show genuine compassion and use the perfect words, and others will say stupid things like, "Can you admit that you were too good for him anyway?" The changes with friendships after a breakup are challenging, and full of stuff that you literally cannot manage. There are a few who will show up and be consistent to support you through this transition, but many will fade when the novelty of the news wears off. This is mainly because they are living their lives and getting back to the status quo.

I have always struggled with the saying, "You know who your true friends are when you are going through something." I have a ton of "friends." I'm a very social person by nature. I

went to two elementary and junior high schools, completed two post-secondary majors, and I aim to complete a third. I have worked in enterprise-level organizations and small businesses. My career, by nature, is to be personal and to connect well with others. I can't remember ever making a new friend along the way and saying, you are awesome—let's be friends and commit to how we will stay together through challenging times. That has never happened. Why? Because we are enjoying our friendship and not trying to fill it with what-ifs.

It is the same with a relationship or marriage—we rarely ever discuss what it would like if we broke up. How many people do you know that have a prenuptial agreement? They are now non-negotiable for me if I were to marry again. If you cannot talk to someone about what it would look like if you broke up, is that not a problem? Shouldn't you be able to talk to them about anything? You discuss what it might be like if you have a kid, or buy a house or car, but you can't talk about the potential of a breakup? Seems strange, right? This is the same with friendships, we don't discuss our expectations with time and yet we expect them to accommodate our changes when shit hits the fan. The fact is they are not obligated. They make a choice, and we must accept that.

How do you manage your friendships post-breakup? You have two options:

1. You tell them what you need and let them respond.
2. You don't manage it and let things play out.

In either scenario, you must be good to yourself and manage your expectations. Ideally, don't have expectations. Some friends will show up and some won't. It is what it is. You can't force someone to be there for you at this moment. It sucks and it's trying. You have changed and they haven't. Generally, people hate change, so when they realize their friend has changed, and they liked the former you who was bubbly, upbeat, and happy, emotionally there is only so much they can handle—especially if they are unable to handle their own emotions. This is part of the reason it is so important, if you can, to quickly get to therapy and join a support group. That is where you will find the people who will understand and support you.

In the meantime, it is fine to keep your distance, especially with those who can't seem to understand that you are processing, adjusting, pivoting, coping, managing, and are simply overwhelmed. It is acceptable to play it by ear and not commit to plans. It is okay to say no every now and then to plans that do not feel good to you. We can only tolerate so much when we are in the stages of healing. We must be kind to ourselves, especially when it feels like those in our world are not. This means setting up boundaries and saying no.

Avoiding Shit Advice

I was mindlessly scrolling through my Facebook feed one day and saw an interview video of the actor and advocate, Terry Crews and his wife Rebecca King-Crews, a southern belle who is gorgeous, classy, poised, and seems very kind. I didn't know what they were going to talk about, but I decided to watch because I was bored. They spoke about infidelity and its aftermath. There was infidelity in their marriage, and it almost caused them to separate. They were candid about this challenging time in their marriage. I was captivated by Rebecca's strength and Terry's transparency and was in awe of how they had gone through such a significant challenge and were able to work through it.

Ms. King-Crews said something with such class and style that has stuck with me to this day. She said, *"Well-meaning people will give you some of the worst advice."* I don't know if it was a quote or her words, but they were the perfect words. They were words that resonated with me, and I know will resonate with you.

I have struggled to find a solid foundation my entire life. I still haven't found one beyond what I have created for myself. There was a lot of chaos during my marriage, and my part in that had to do with my career and striving for more. There was also a lot of financial chaos. But my kids, thank God, had a foundation. They had roots. They came home from the hospital to a house that they still, to this day, live in. My oldest son was 11 years old as I wrote this. By the time I was his age, I had already moved at least 12 times. Imagine...I moved more times than the years I had lived. That is utter chaos—instability is chaos in your mind. I always knew I was going to find a foundation. I genuinely believe you can't progress in life without a solid foundation, whether it's provided for you, or you create it.

If we look at Maslow's Hierarchy of Needs, which represents what we need to go from surviving to thriving, the basic psychological needs are food, shelter, water, clothing, and sleep. The next level is safety. You can only move up to this level if your basic psychological needs are met. This level includes security of body, employment, resources, morality, family, and health. This level is the foundation one truly needs. These things are as stable as they can be. In a bad economy, employment may go, but if you keep your property, you remain stable. However, if you lose that as well, you may be living in bad circumstances.

The next level, after safety is taken care of, is love and belonging. This level is about friendship, family, and sexual intimacy. This is where we find connection and peace. There are two other levels of the hierarchy (esteem and self-actualization), but I'll stop at love and belonging because this book is about healing from the level you are probably most challenged by right now. Your friendships have changed because you have changed. Your family situation has changed if you are divorced, especially if you have kids. Let's face it unless you are fortunate, the intimacy/sex area is lacking. As I write this chapter, it has been over a year and a half without sex, and trust me, not because I want it that way. Healing during a pandemic is to blame for this one.

Where am I going with this? No matter what level you currently inhabit, if its foundation is falling apart, you feel like you are losing things. You may be going down a level rather than moving up. This is challenging. At this time, you will be a target for well-meaning advice that more than likely does not serve you. But you are searching. You need solutions, you need resolutions.

No one, except for one of my aunts, wanted me to fight for my marriage. Everyone around me said, "Move on, you are better than he is anyway." I was incredibly saddened by that reality. I had a home where people were invited in. I often served food. We were supportive people, and when my marriage died, I heard "you are better" and "you are strong and will be better." No one seemed to champion my marriage which to me, was gross and sad. I have never suggested leaving to anyone who has come to me for advice about their marriage, even if I hated their spouse's guts. Especially when there were children involved. But it is strange and amazing how others will put on you what they wish they could do.

With this said, be very mindful of the advice you receive. Filter the good shit, and let's face it, shit is rarely good. People have a lot to say, and you never know what is driving the engine behind what they have to say. If they are angry and cannot regulate that emotion, they will say stupid shit. If they are sad and cannot regulate that emotion, they will say stupid shit. You might be in a place where you are very vulnerable which means that being able to filter good and bad advice is hard. Find ways to manage the advice you receive without completely sheltering yourself from the world.

Being Your Own Hero

"...but darling, in the end, you've got to be your own hero, because everybody's busy trying to save themselves"

~ C.T.

I remember walking into my kid's school to pick him up. I only went to the school because I had to speak to one of the teachers about the divorce. At this point, my kids didn't know about the divorce in the works, however, I was certain they knew something was up and I was concerned their teachers were taking the brunt of it. I walked to my youngest son's classroom. He was busy putting on his shoes because it was the end of the day. I had a brief, swift moment to talk to his teacher. She and I had a great relationship, and we were always excited to see each other. I asked her if she had a moment and for me, she always does. I said what I need to tell you must be quick, and I need your help to discuss this with the school counsellor and my older son's teacher. She was visibly worried and very attentive—she knew it was serious.

I let her know that my husband and I were divorcing, that the kids were unaware— but knew that something was off—

and this was something I felt she should know. If they were acting up in class—she confirmed my younger son was doing so—I requested that they be given a lot more compassion and understanding. She assured me this was not going to be an issue, gave me her condolences, and I walked away. It was quick.

That was a very frequent thing that happened at that time. I had to be brave and inform those people who I felt needed to know. The shock from everyone confirmed and validated my current state. But I had to move forward and get "in formation" as Beyoncé would say, for the sake of the kids. In the process, I realized I was being my kids' hero and by the time their dad moved out and they were informed, I was burnt out from being a hero to others and not to myself. There is a lot you must face when you realize you need to be your own hero, especially facing the label of being divorced.

When I became part of the "divorce club", I felt I had a label, and it is not elite. It's like the grocery store discount sticker on a bag of veggies about to expire the next day. At least, that is how I felt. Others have described something similar, and it summed up that they felt discounted or devalued in many ways. Our cost, our value, has been reduced in our minds. In our anger, sadness, and disappointment, we speak discounted words. This happens when we speak poorly about the spouse. This happens when we complain about our circumstances. This happens when we say we cannot _____ (fill in the blank). We speak in a way that discounts us. When we do this, feel this way, speak this way, we start planting a seed of negativity in our minds. It doesn't help that we might feel negative already. We do not do this on purpose—it's not our intention. The point is, when trauma hits, and believe me, divorce or a sudden breakup is a trauma, we are not okay. We are not ourselves. We cannot think properly. Our brains are not processing well. Also, we're tired. Emotional exhaustion is one of the worst types of exhaustion. We just want to be heard. So, when we are given an opportunity to talk, we tend to spin out of control and overshare. Again, therapy is important. Having someone you can trust who will sit with you at any time is important. It's important to have someone who is willing to validate you and coach you to be wary of what you say and to whom. That would be a perfect world, however, you will likely have to dig deep and become your own hero. You are angry, sad, and hurt, but you don't have to be mentally incarcerated, too. Allowing yourself to journey into your own mental jail, which is burning and holds bad feelings, ill will, and negative tongues is not going to serve you. The hero is in you.

In one of the last episodes of *Game of Thrones*, one of the fan favourites was Arya. She emerged as a strong hero who went through a lot to be groomed to radiate strength. And yet, in the final season, she was faced with what looked like defeat. In fact, she is the toughest character. She had endured several storms throughout this series and rose like a phoenix every time. In one scene, it looked as though the evil Night King had won. There was no way anyone was going to defeat him. There was a scene with Arya and this evil witch in which she turned to Arya and said, "You know what you need to do." Arya looked at her and said, "Right." Anyone watching would assume that meant she was to sacrifice herself to try and defeat the Night King. She had to go to the battle line and face him. This is what she did. She was, even in her darkest hour, not done fighting yet. Even weary, drained, and broken, she was not done. In a suspenseful scene, Arya approached the battle line where she faced the Night King and she was victorious, remaining a hero. Moments after that show aired, this character lit up social media. No one had to say anything, they just posted her picture. It was an unspoken, no spoiler moment for everyone. See, you are Arya. In your darkest hour, in your moment of defeat, in your tired body, you are a hero. You just have to say "Right," turn around, walk towards the mountain or the battlefield and fight for yourself!

Owning Your Worth

"He who has a why can bear any how."

~ Friedrich Nietzsche

In September 2019, I had to activate an aggressive job search because I wasn't far away from financial annihilation. I was intent on keeping the home in which I had raised my kids. I had moved over 17 times by the time I graduated from high school. There is something to be said about roots, foundation, knowing where you come from. My kids may never fully appreciate it, but I know— giving them continuity through the house is huge.

All my bills were doubling quickly. I paid for the mortgage for most of the marriage, but the utilities, groceries, and more were covered by my ex. Now I was taking care of everything on my own. My state of overwhelm was beginning to show up in my body. I was breaking out in what looked like chickenpox on my right arm and upper back. My doctor wanted to put them in the category of shingles, but they weren't, they were another symptom of all the stress I was holding. I could have chosen to let the house go, but I work hard, and I was ready to give it all I had. I couldn't give up without a fight.

The mortgage was at the same amount as when it was purchased due to debt, over the years, which was tied into the mortgage. This was not something I wanted and yet I never really felt there was a choice. At this point, I had just completed my contract and was out of work. The first time I was ever out of work as a single woman, except now I had two children and a home.

For seven years of my career, I was a career coach, however, as the saying goes, those who teach don't do. It is not uncommon for a chef to not cook at home, or for a professional sports coach to pass on coaching their kids. It's a need for balance. For approximately the past eight years, I hadn't needed to actively search for a job. I was always approached. I had a great network and people who enjoyed working with me or who wanted to work with me in the future, but this was a particularly challenging market. Jobs were not a dime a dozen. Especially for those "nice to have" skills in which I excelled. Nice to have skills to fill a role in a company that they know they need, but they are not seen as valuable as the finance team.

I was a Career and Talent Specialist. My focuses were Career Coaching, Talent Development, Learning and Development, and Talent Acquisition. I had to tap into any skills I had, apply them, and pray for support along the way. My heart was still broken. I was crushed and drained emotionally. I felt deflated as if I was a depreciated asset. It all brought me down during this time, and I was quickly losing hope.

I remember sitting on the floor of my room, writing in my journal the list of pros if I ended my life. I felt that with my kids going between homes, having to potentially move again if I lost the house, and possibly having a stepparent or two was too much to bear. I had done everything I could to avoid this situation. I said that divorce was not an option when I got married, but inevitably it was not my decision. In writing all of this in the journal, I came up with enough pros that I set a date. It was supposed to be in January 2020. I cannot bring myself to read it now because being reminded that I was in such a dark place at one point is a lot to handle. I am a happy, fun, loving person, and I was lower than low. I was going to work my ass off to find work and my goal was to keep the house. If I knew what would happen next, I think the only thing I can say is that there was divine intervention.

One of my best friends in Toronto was probably on the phone with me every day for weeks. She reviewed all my applications for grammatical errors and gave me daily pep talks. She knew I was low and took it upon herself to be that support. My dad had my back as best as he could, too. Within six weeks I not only found a job, but I also found one that paid me more than what I wanted, with a great company, great team and boss, flexibility, and exciting projects.

When the lockdowns began for COVID-19 a couple of months later, I was able to put my mortgage on hold to save a bit of money and pay down some debt. I am 100 per cent sure that the prayers I said every morning and the actions I took delivered this result. I wanted to give up and throw in the towel so badly, but my reason why was strong enough to continue to try—my kids, their stability, their love, and their lives. Yes, I was at a point where I thought they were better off without me, but I am sure many people have felt that way. I dug deep, prayed hard, and rose high. But I was not alone. The cost was almost huge but eventually, before I found work, I reconnected with my value and arose to meet the challenges before me.

Divorce or breakups are not cheap. They come with major costs that no one factors into their budget. The emotional taxes paid on a breakup is huge. But there are also dividing assets, which should be called depreciating assets. As a couple, especially a couple that may have been moderately responsible with money, you go from having a full house, to selling and downsizing. You go from new cars with manageable payments to a used car that may need repairs you more than likely cannot afford. You go from a health pension and an investment plan to barely anything at all since many need to pull from that money to get back to a financial starting line again. You go from having people who claim to love you, to watching them vanish overnight, never checking on you. You go from abundance to loss. It's no wonder people become hateful, spiteful, resentful, deflated, and discouraged after a breakup.

Life may be tough. You may feel unappreciated. Please know that your value is not determined by being in a relationship, having a big house, and a fancy car. Your value is not based on you being the size of your investments. Those are nice-to-have assets. Your value is based on your character—who you are as a person. When all this was happening to me, a friend inadvertently offered me a lifeline when she commented, "If you don't think people are not watching or seeing you rise, you are wrong. People are very proud of you and see you." That was huge.

Are you a good person? Are you trying to make life happen for you in challenging times? Do you have a good, kind heart? Are you a positive, contributing member of society? Do people appreciate you in their lives? Do you show up to work and put in your fair share? Do you pay your taxes? The point I am making here is that if you are trying, you are showing up. It may be hard, you may feel like you lack value, but you are being watched. People see you. People are admiring you. You are worth more than you know.

Resisting Revenge, It Is Not Sweet

After I had my first son, I felt very alone. I didn't enjoy the isolation. I went into a state of postpartum sadness quite quickly and I struggled. I had no community. I had no one with whom I felt connected as I went through this new experience. I loved, loved, loved my baby, but felt very isolated. I didn't know what to do half the time. He was a baby who only wanted to be held and never wanted to be put down. He always wanted to be in someone's arms—my arms. We were instant besties except that one bestie was nursing, not sleeping, had many needs, and I, as per usual, gave up myself to ensure this person—the most important person in my world at this time—had his needs met.

By the time he was seven months, I felt I was going crazy. I had no friends who were at home with their babies, and I wanted to get out way more. Spring was upon us, and I knew that also had something to do with it. I found myself a therapist to express some of my thoughts to and to work through things. Turns out, I had a lot to work out. She is still my therapist to this day, 11 years later.

I also started going to more play spaces. I was by myself, but I thought it would be good for his socialization as well.

It was amazing and interesting to notice how many people, mainly moms, start up conversations with you. All it took was for one baby to show interest in your baby and suddenly, moms were connected as if by osmosis. One time, I met a woman I really liked. We agreed to meet once a week since she too was home most of the time. Our conversations were surface-level small talk, but good. We both knew when to giggle, when to say something sarcastic, and we were both non-judgmental. At least that is what I thought.

About the fourth time we met up, she seemed agitated. I get that, when you are a new mom, sleepless nights can get you there. I asked her how she was doing, and she just unleashed, "One of my friends just had a baby and is really struggling." "Well, that is awesome, right?" I responded. She looked straight ahead, but her eyes went a bit sadistically dark, and she replied, "Yes, it's great. Now she will know how tough it is and I won't be there for her like she wasn't there for me." I was a bit floored and didn't know how to respond. In fact, at the time, with my nursing-mom brain (a non-functioning one), I didn't respond at all. I swiftly changed the subject. That was the last time I saw that woman. I went back to the play space the following week but didn't see her. I assumed that she, too, felt that what she'd said was a bit wrong. But I get it.

So, what does this have to do with a breakup? We all tend to have a moment where we want revenge. Where we feel like we need answers, especially if we are the ones left behind. We tend to have a sadistic moment. Anger, as I have mentioned previously, is not healthy. Resentment is the twin sister of anger and that too is unhealthy. Doing this will never help you move forward. You will never have peace. I have seen this happen so many times and it serves no one. I have seen friends hop in their cars and go to their ex's house and stalk them. I have seen people befriend someone just to get closer to this person to piss off their ex. In my 20s, I almost slept with someone close to the guy that hurt me. I stopped myself before it could happen, but even the fact that I was in that moment of revenge made me feel sick.

I implore you to truly understand that revenge does nothing for anything. There are several ways this plays out. Many people lean on karma, thinking that is going to take care of the other person. Do not do it. Karma is a boomerang, and if you wish ill will on someone else, once they receive that boomerang, it comes back to you. So, do not do it.

- Don't drive in front of their house.
- Don't slash their tires.
- Don't smash their car with a bat.
- Don't tell their family or friends about the horrible things they did.
- Don't leave nasty messages on their machine.

When these thoughts cross your mind, let them cross, and move on. Force your mind to visualize yourself stepping out of the current scene and watch it as you would a spectator looking at a train wreck in shock. Know that it is not you. It is not healthy to be acting out of rage. However, it is healthy and normal to think the thoughts—we all have at some point. Go home or for a drive in your car and yell out loud. Keep a rock or stress ball with you and grasp it tight every time you feel rage. No one desires to live in regret and this where you will be if you take any actions like those pointed out above. It only feels good for a moment, but then you feel bad when you come to and realize what you have done. Trust me.

"The best revenge is enjoying life without them." I don't know who wrote this, but it struck me when I saw it. This could not be truer. When your ex hears, sees, or knows you are happy, that is the best revenge. Why? If you are genuinely happy, you no longer care. You are disconnected from that person. They will feel that, and they won't like it. Even if they are in a new relationship. There is something about people wanting what they cannot have. Suddenly it looks new, bright, and shiny.

Just know that this will be the only sweet revenge. The sweet part is that you don't care about how it is affecting them because you are enjoying what you have. At that moment, you no longer care what they think, feel, and want.

Resisting the Urge to Punish

I shared a story earlier about my dad and my stepmom breaking up. It was the second abandonment, maybe the third. I had a person who claimed to care about me—the first being my mother—though through no fault of her own if mental illness is that much of an uncontrollable spiral. The second would be the woman my dad had us move in with after we left my mom. This stepmom of seven years would be the next. I felt like I was losing it. I had so much going on in that year—expulsion from school just a couple of months from Grade Nine graduation— chickenpox about a month before Grade Nine—my parents' breakup and then several moves after that. You can throw in a second expulsion when I was kicked out of my school the second week of Grade Ten. I felt like I had no one who truly cared.

I saw others, my friends, whose moms were putting up with their bullshit and still loving them, but I could not seem to hold one female role model in my life. No one seemed to find it within them to stick by me. I look back and know that was it. I knew that was what I needed. That need was unleashing an unhealthy beast—an angry girl who just couldn't give a shit. I had a few scraps, some that were worth it, others I had no means starting. I was skipping school, not caring about much. It seemed that no one was giving me—a child—a lifeline. Could the principals of those schools not recognize that my postal

154

code kept changing? Could the teachers not recognize that I wasn't bathing? The signs of a girl in distress were there and no one stood up. I was too young and hormonal to figure that out on my own. But when I became an adult, I did. I knew that the lessons from those experiences had to be quickly learned.

One thing I learned from those experiences was that I was not going to punish someone else for the hurt those people caused me. When I got that down, when I got it in my head to not punish someone else for what another person did, I felt the universe test me with more trials that almost broke me. It was like I was being tested over and over, approximately every seven years, to see if I understood how I should react, or what I should do. While I am never sure I have passed the test because this has happened more than I would like, I do know that punishment should be aimed at the right person.

I have been an adult now for 25 years. I have seen so many people punish the wrong person because they believed they caused them pain. I saw a guy verbally abuse his wife because he never dealt with his real issues. I saw a girl cheat on her man, over and over, because she never addressed the pain the guy who hurt her, caused. I saw another person use a person for kindness with zero regard for their feelings because getting too close to someone seemed toxic compared to the norm they were used to.

Managing Setbacks

As I am writing this, I am coming off a setback. Nope, not sex with the ex or anything like that, but it was a two-week setback with my emotions. I am not sure what the first trigger was. Was it the huge car bill? Was it the bill for the dryer that was double the quoted amount? Was it witnessing a friend struggling with a family member dying? Was it the most recent interrogation from one of my sons wanting to know why their father and I really divorced, in addition to being devastated that I was spending Thanksgiving alone (which I hadn't told him, but he assumed)? Was it the struggles I was having at work because I was emotionally and mentally drained from 2019 and 2020, which had hit me like a ton of bricks? I will guess it is all the above. But what happened was a setback. I felt like I was back to the day I was dumped. I felt like I was in the *Groundhog Day* movie except nothing looked the same—only how I was feeling was the same. I was in shock, denial, and crying way too often to understand what these small triggers—minute compared to the year before—were causing me to have a slight breakdown. So, what did I do to manage this?

I scheduled a weekly call with one of my besties in Toronto. This is something I have done since the divorce announcement, one of my go-to strategies. I had the safety and trust of someone that I could say "I need a call stat" to and know they would make the time. I also requested an appointment with my therapist to have some backup emotional support. Both people reminded me of what I had achieved up to this point. They both validated my feelings and were proud of what I had accomplished. They gave me positive reinforcement while listening to my pain and frustration.

Setbacks happen. Everyone will have a different trigger. This time, my trigger led to the need to be heard and to vent. I knew it, felt it, acted on it. You must use the tools you have gained in this book to help you manage those setbacks. Will you call someone? Will you journal? Will you go for a run? Will you meditate or pray? The options are endless. One tip I found in a *Psychology Today* article titled, "9 Strategies to Manage a Personal Setback" by Dr. David Susman, a Recovery Coach, and Ph.D., was to "know it will not last forever" and plan 20-minute setback breaks. The goal is to work through the impact of that setback quickly so you can move forward.

The probability of a setback is high. It is just the nature of life. But we can have a proactive plan to manage these setbacks, a plan you know will work for you. My practice, incorporating several elements from this book, is to have a happy list. This is a list that is a go-to plan to help manage setbacks, upsets, frustrations, and times when I'm sad. It is a list that helps me to get unstuck and out of my rut. I encourage you to complete the next exercise and create a list that will help you quickly navigate a setback.

EXERCISE

1.   Open your Notes app on your phone or create a list on a page in your journal.

2.   Create a Laugh file. Did you know that laughter is medicine? It has been proven to increase your immune system, lower stress, and reduce pain. When we are in a funk from a setback, we need this to help climb out of the funk.

     a.   Choose three to five go-to things that will make you laugh.
     b.   To get ideas, consider going to YouTube and searching your favourite comedians' clips and save them in a "laughter" folder on your browser. Or go to Netflix for favourite key stand-ups or sitcoms you know are a guaranteed laugh.
     c.   Add these things to your main happy list.

3.   Identify key friends you can call.

     a.   Identify two to three friends you know you can text and/or call to say, "Emergency, I need to talk" and they will know to get on the phone with you immediately.

b. Flag them as favourites on your phone.

c. Write their names on the list.

d. Give them a heads-up (in case they don't know).

4. Make a smile photo album.

    a. Go to the key sources where your photos are stored (your phone, computer, or social media platforms).

    b. Review some pictures that make you smile.

    c. For every photo you find, do as follows depending on what your plan is:

        i. If you plan to make an actual physical album, click, and save them all in the same file. I suggest using your computer to create a file and save them there as it is easier to create and order your photo album.

        ii. If you plan to make a photo album on your phone, you need to save the pictures to your phone, but make sure to save them to your album too. If there is a slight chance that is not working, then save them to a new note on your phone. Many people don't know you can do this, but you can save pictures to a note file on your phone. You can also lock that note if you like.

    d. Make a note on your list that this photo album exists and where it is.

5. Make a list of your favourite spots.

    a. Do you have a favourite ice cream place?
    b. Do you have a favourite bookstore?
    c. Do you have a place to walk or look at the scenery?
    d. Where is your favourite place to watch people?

6. Make a list of your following favourites:

    a. Movie(s)
    b. Book(s)
    c. Show(s) to binge-watch.

The goal is to have a go-to list, ready and waiting, for when you might need it. Look at the list when you need to and take it one step further— share it with a friend so they know what your go-to is. Then they can remind you in case you forget.

Knowing the Truth about Sex with the Ex

My 20s were rough years when it came to like, love, and lust. I got all three confused regularly and don't know how I kept my head above water. I dove into relationships so fast, hoping to find something solid, and chose men who were all wrong for me. I can admit it. The following is the best story I have, to share with you for this chapter.

I was out at a nightclub one night with friends, taking a much-needed study break. My school and work combination had left me more isolated than social. Since I had been working out a lot at that time too, I was looking polished and together. We went to this great club just outside of our downtown core. The music there was always a great mix of the 90s and early 2000s RnB and hip hop. The place was full of the usual club suspects that you would see every time—the fresh recruits for the local football team that you knew were from the finest parts of the USA, and dabblers in this world. We were transitioning usual suspects. We were not bar stars anymore. We only went out once or twice a month as we transitioned into discovering other interests.

He was tall, handsome, and successful. It was clear as day that he was all three, right away. Best of all, he was interested in me. He asked me to dance, and although his moves were almost embarrassing, he was trying. Then he bought me a cocktail or two, we had a good chat, exchanged numbers, and away we went. He called me the next morning. He was on it. While I was taken by his charm, he was someone I was hesitant about. Maybe it was because he was a little more mature than me; maybe his charm was more polished than what I was used to. I was also in school full-time and working full-time, so bringing someone into my life at that moment was probably not a great idea. I was stressed to the maximum and needed to keep my eye on the prize, which was finishing my degree and keeping my amazing job. Falling in love, or lust, or like was just not on my to-do list at the time.

He laid it on thick for the first two weeks and planned a date with me every three days. He called me to see how I was doing at least once a day. He was persistent. One night he wanted to plan a night out with me, but I had already made plans with friends. I knew that it was not smart to cancel with my friends so I let him know where I would be and that he would be more than welcome to join us. This way I could let my friends size him up. He joined us. He met us at the pricey tapas house we frequented. I'm not sure why any of us felt we could afford this lifestyle, but we attempted to. I let my friends know that he might join us, and they were excited to meet him. After all, everyone had been impressed with my date stories about him so far.

When he arrived, he was wearing his best clothes and looked amazing. I tell you—clothes do make the man. He looked hot

 162

and my friends took notice right away. He was engaged in our conversations and chatted with everyone there, with or without me by his side. He was attentive to me as well throughout the night. He checked everyone's approval boxes and I left with him that night to go to his house.

This man was charming, handsome, successful, charismatic, and clean (his place was immaculate). I was about to find out that he was very good in the bedroom as well. That is what got me fully interested—the sex. He was exceptional at what he did and the sex, on top of it all, was more than icing on the cake.

As the weeks went by, our dates started to lessen, and although sex was still on the schedule, another side of him started to surface. There was a very guarded and possibly angry man in there. Maybe he was scared to fall in love, maybe he was stressed with work, but I didn't know and wasn't really in the mood to find out. He was different and wouldn't communicate with me about what was going on with him. Pretty quickly, we started seeing each other less and officially broke it off about five months after we started dating. Two weeks after we broke it off, he sent me a late-night text. We all know what that means. I needed some stress relief and really, I did not like him more than that anyways. Or so I thought. I arrived at his place, and he had my favourite wine there, trying to create a nice ambience. He told me everything I wanted to hear—how he was sorry and how he was scared, and blah, blah, blah. I was putty and we ended up sleeping together. In the morning, he was cold towards me again. I was embarrassed and sad that I fell for it. Never again, and never did I, again.

Sex with the ex is easily summed up for you in three words: DON'T DO IT!

Why? Five reasons:
1. You will get confused.
2. You will probably regret it.
3. Short-term gain for long-term pain—sex, on average, lasts seven minutes. That is seven minutes of gain for maybe two to three months of pain. Not worth it.
4. You want to move forward, and this rarely means looking back for too long. Constantly taking that step back, only sets you back.
5. Hope—you want hope, not to lose hope—hope for your future, your rehabilitated self-esteem, and hope for bigger and better things—could be compromised by this move.

Now that I have that out of the way, let me explain why and the fact is, there is no grey area in this. People make every excuse in the book to justify sex with the ex, such as:

-   *I really needed it.* Well, you know what? I really need a million dollars, but I am not going to rob a small bank to get it.
-   *I really needed to see if I was over him/her.* I would really love to know who killed JFK. I would love to know the Caramilk secret. I would also love to know if there are aliens in our universe. But some things are better left alone.
-   *I have needs!* The need for sex is indeed included on Abraham Maslow's Hierarchy of Needs pyramid, but nowhere does it say you have to have sex with

the ex. There are millions of single people in North America. MILLIONS. There is a pretty good chance you will find at least one to have sex with. Acknowledge that in this case, sex is a want, not a need. You want to move forward, not backward, and this a big leap back.

❧ *I was drunk.* Not going to lie, I have been there, back in my 20s. Being intoxicated can put you in a vulnerable position. Your judgment is flawed. You are emotional. Check out the hundreds of drunk-girl memes on Instagram. They will show you how we "think we act" and how we are really acting. Until your head is in a healthy and strong place, it's best to know your limit and stay within it. You know not to drink and drive so know not to drink and have sex with the ex.

❧ *I didn't want another notch on my belt.* This is the best excuse I've heard yet. Honey, this is pride speaking. No one needs to know but you and your maker. The person you're having sex with doesn't think of you as someone who is getting another notch on their belt. Women are now at an all-time high for empowerment and liberation. But if you don't feel comfortable with that notch, don't have sex. Abstain. Additionally, sometimes a partner will see one person as one too many. A secure person will never ask you how many people you have slept with. An insecure person will ask you only because they are scared or insecure and feel they could be compared to someone else. There is no need to let anyone know.

Every process you have gone through so far has helped you to heal, got you out of bed, made you take a shower, shave your legs, or trim your crazy eyebrows. Everything up until now has put you in a position to move forward. So why take ten giant steps back? That is what sex with the ex is—ten giant steps back.

You cannot convince yourself it is just sex. You are going to be fooling yourself. In addition, the only person crying, hurting, and feeling deflated afterwards, is you. You know you still have feelings for that person, which is why you are so willing to engage in a bedroom delight. If you didn't have feelings for that person and it was 'just sex', the last person you would want it with is the person who broke your heart. If you were over it, and it was 'just sex' the last person you would be able to perform with is the person who broke your heart. I know that at this point, you want more and are trying to move forward, remember?

What to do when the urge/opportunity arises:

1. Just say no. Like drugs, this one is not good for you.
2. Take a cold shower. The temporary pain is much less than the roller-coaster feeling you go on after sleeping with the ex. A three-minute shower should do it.
3. Go to the gym. Use your pent-up energy. Possibly meet someone new. Again, this is short-term pain, with massive rewards.
4. Get out of the house. Surround yourself with other things and people. Get your mind off the problem.
5. Get a toy. You know what I mean. This could offend some people and I won't apologize for it. It is a billion-dollar industry. This will be your little secret that keeps you safe and away from the ex. You can shop online, contact a local passion party expert, or go to a store. If you bring this topic up with friends, there

will be some who are bold enough to admit they have toys, some who are shy about them, or not open to discussing them. The thing is, deep down, you may have a problem sleeping with your ex. The repercussions of that problem are causing your head to spin. The only thing that should spin is the toy you have. You know exactly what the outcome is after using a toy. You also know the disastrous outcome of sleeping with your ex. The toy will not play mind games with you after. The toy will not screw up your self-esteem. The toy will not treat you like a dirty little secret.

Now, I get that sometimes your ex is a great individual, but the two of you together, in a committed relationship is not the right fit. Sometimes you have both come to that conclusion together but enjoy the sex in the meantime until you find a better fit for your life. If you can have an honest conversation with one another, lay out the rules. If you cannot commit to not expecting more or are challenged with the arrangement, then move forward. I do not know of many of these situations. The only one I have known of and admired, turned out to be a lie. One person was hoping the other would come around, kept it a secret, and then got frustrated after a few months.

Cycling Through the Yo-Yo Effects

"The people who truly know and love you, know your weaknesses but will never take advantage of them. They will see your flaws and never judge them."

~ Unknown

Have you ever seen the unhealthy relationship someone has with one who is stringing them along? Back and forth, back, and forth—you feel like you are watching a relationship Groundhog Day. The one person has the power and baits the other one to come in—either for a night at a time, or a week at a time, or even a month. Then they are finished again, only to have to hear days or months later they are trying that relationship again. It's super frustrating to watch and even more frustrating to be tangled in. The term is called Relationship Cycling. I don't know the true source of that name, but I read an article entitled "The Gloomy Psychology of 'Relationship Cycling'" by Cari Room, written for The Cut. When you are the one in this yo-yo relationship, you are the one who loses pieces of yourself through every cycle of the relationship. It is unhealthy for your mental state and does not serve you.

Sometimes people like to play with your mind. They will break up with you and then still string you along for a while. They will text you randomly, "checking in." They may even like and comment on your social media posts. They might send you a meme, gif, or joke you may like. They may ask you to go to dinner every now and then and act like it is normal when it just might be to temporarily solve their boredom. Do not let them play with your head. Do not let them play with your emotions. Do not let them play with your heart. Go to the bathroom; look at your back in the mirror. If there are no strings on your back, then you have now confirmed you are not a yo-yo or a puppet on a string. Do not let anyone keep pulling on your non-existent strings. An ex will come in and out when you let them. Their emotions change to cater to them, while yours stay the same. But when they do this, they are yo-yo-ing you. Pulling you in, pushing you away. It's not fair, it's not right, and it's not what you want. So, let's get rid of the problem.

How do we do this?

1. If they call, don't answer the phone! Simple! You know how to screen phone calls. You know when your mom calls and she's probably going to nag you about something, you will not pick up the phone. You know when that negative friend you dread talking to—because it is all about them all the time—and you have learned the art of not picking up the phone with them. So, why can't you do this with the person who has hurt you the most? If you can screen the calls of your loved ones, people who only want the best for you, especially the

one who gave birth to you—trust me you can screen the phone calls of the person who left you and made it hard for you to get out of bed. Change their ID in your phone to "This person will hurt me" and you will be reminded not to pick up.

2. If you see them while out and they seem to be talking close to you, drawing you in, feeding you compliments (of course they are because if you have been practising the stuff in this book, you look amazing), tell them you are on a tight schedule and must get back to what you were doing. Even if what you were doing was nothing.

3. If your friends say they have run into him, and he asked them to tell you to call him—this is a smooth tactic. Let's give that person a slow clap and a bottle of Canadian Whiskey; however, don't confirm this information with your friend by saying "Really"?—And then following that up with "What did he say?"—because they just told you what he said. Don't ask, "So how did he say it, did he seem sad we are over?" or anything silly like that. Does it look like he has regrets? WHO CARES!!! If there wasn't some form of sincere attempt from him five months ago to get you back, then something tells me this is not much of a sincere attempt. It is smooth, trust me, but we are not all dealing with Mr. Big from *Sex & The City*. This story rarely ends up like that, so let it go. If you are unfamiliar, after years of amazing and not so amazing moments between Carrie Bradshaw (main character) and Mr. Big, they finally ended up together. Just say to your friends, "Thanks for letting me know," and pivot the conversation. Trust me, you will earn some serious respect points. If they ask you what you are going to do, let them know you don't

know, you might think about it, but right now you want to focus on being with the people you are with at this moment.

The challenge with going on a cycling mission with someone is that no one has truly learned how to solve problems. You just know to fly the moment things get rough, uncomfortable, boring, or for any typical relationship challenge. This is toxic and serves you in no way. Aim to know you deserve more and demand more. It is not acceptable. You deserve more.

Dating When You're Ready

It was a lovely summer afternoon. I was waiting for my friend on this riverside bike path in our city. I always looked forward to getting together with her because we have the best chats. Bicycling is new in my life. When I was young, I flew over my handlebars and landed face-first on the pavement. While I was lucky to not have lost any teeth, I fractured my jaw and broke my right wrist. I became fearful of bikes—completely idiotic considering it wasn't the bike that caused the accident, it was the rowdy preteen who wanted to ride with no hands while riding full speed down a hill that needed some TLC from our city's construction team.

Our bike ride started at a spot I knew well. I had just finished running my first 5 km race there a year before in August 2019, just two months after the divorce announcement. I look back now and pat myself on the back for that one.

The day was gorgeous, and the paths were filled with riders and walkers. The trees were so full, with that perfect number of leaves that let you know that you need to appreciate this moment because in a blink the seasons will change. The river was crowded with floaters and paddle boaters. The nearby streets were filled with heavier traffic than I had seen since before the pandemic. Everyone was being nice. My friend and I

rode beside each other (she rode on the grass) so that we could talk. Like normal, we covered a gazillion topics in less than an hour. We were getting close to taking a pub break and the topic of my dating life came up. "So, how is the dating game going for you," she asked nervously. "I have decided that right now I really have to work on me," I responded calmly and with full assurance. "But I am not saying this in an 'I need to work on myself to avoid dating because I am scared' cover-up. I am scared, there is no doubt, but I also know that this has hit me hard. I also know that this pandemic is not a time to kiss new people." I did see it as an opportunity because I also knew what I wanted. It was so clear that I had it written on seven pages in my large journal. I later wrote it again and it was almost identical to the original one—I knew what I wanted. I had to ask myself, was I ready for that person? Was I as active as I wanted to be? Were my finances in order as much as they would need to be for someone to be in my life and not run in the other direction? No! The list went on. Some of it was good to go, but other parts were not.

I am not talking about perfection, but I am talking about mirroring and showing up in alignment. I know I am looking for a partner, not a prince on a white horse. I want someone to walk with, not someone who wants to save a damsel in distress. One, I am not that damsel, and two, fairy tales are for children. I would say, if the perfect man showed up on my doorstep tomorrow, I would not be silly. I guess maybe I would explore it if it were convenient. Very convenient. I do not find apps convenient right now—too much effort and low return for most people I know.

Everyone you know wants to see you happy. They want to see you living your best life, but that doesn't mean you have to dive into a relationship right away. You may believe you are ready, and I think that is great. Tap into that. Are you diving in out of fear or for your image, or are you sincerely ready?

If you are ready, then read below.

I don't want to mislead you. I am not against dating. If you are ready, trust me, I have done my due diligence here.

I reconnected with a friend recently who I haven't seen in years. We were able to make plans to go for cocktails. When I saw her, it was like no time had passed except that our embrace was proof it had. We dove right into talking and catching up quickly to that day. I love reconnecting with people with whom you feel like no time has passed. You may have both gone through a lot over the years and may not be aware of it, but you will catch up with no love loss for not being there for each other and have some awesome laughs. We met up at 6:30 p.m. and didn't stop talking, laughing, drinking, and eating until 2:00 a.m. It was great.

She shared her wedding story and showed me her pictures. With her Middle Eastern beauty, she was a stunning bride. The groom was not hard on the eyes either. I told her about my divorce. She asked me if I planned to date, and I said I wasn't sure. I struggled with the thought. Having two impressionable sons, I wanted them to have exposure to a healthy loving relationship but was also not looking to be a revolving door trying to find "the one." It was confusing and frustrating. That sparked her to speak some truth to me. "Listen, you are in the most opportune time for yourself," she said very matter-of-factly. "I don't know why you don't see it," she continued. She didn't care that I was in shock from her response. "You're doing well by yourself which is great. You don't need to share bills with someone. You are calling the shots. You are not in a rush. You can choose to date someone for as long as you like before you ever introduce them to your kids. You can be fully transparent about your priorities, and no one will disrespect them because they will get that your kids are number one. If they don't, say goodbye." She stopped talking and raised an eyebrow saying, "Bring on your rebuttal." I had nothing. I replied, "I think you are right. I never thought about it that way." She let down the war armour her body language was sending me. I asked, "So, how do I do this? I am fearful of apps and it's COVID-19, so next to impossible to meet people right now." She explained to me that I needed to know what I wanted, and I needed to stand my ground. Because online dating or dating, in general, will be a journey, you must know what you want. Focus on the journey and what you learn about yourself in the process. Try not to let yourself be swayed, because you will. You will want to give up and settle. You will want to find chemistry and follow it.

She told me to choose an app and stick with it, and to be realistic that not everyone is a "one and done." I may have to meet 15 people before I find one with whom I connect. I may have to meet more than that or less. But I had to stick with one app and go with it. She continued to share stories from multiple friends who have gone down this road. I listened to her stories and took some that I gathered from other friends to come up with the how-to date-on-an-app list.

1. Choose an app that you feel is right for you. Turns out there are apps that are more inclined to attract certain age brackets versus others. Also, some apps do better in some area codes than others. I don't want to sway anyone to any app so please research this or best, listen to others. My only advice is to know what you want.

2. Create a great profile. Here's how you do this:

   a. Ask a few of your friends to tell you what they feel are your best qualities, what your values are, and several other self-awareness questions. You will see a consistent message which should be what you put in your profile.

   b. Make sure you are positive in writing this profile. Do not put things like "I have no time for..." or "Don't bother messaging me if..." Just focus on the positive and trust in yourself that you can weed out people you do not want.

   c. Write your profile in as few words as possible, condensing all of this. It's tough, but worth it. Many people will only read so much.

3. Take a few great, natural pictures (no filters). Grab a friend, buy them a coffee, put on a nice outfit, and take a few pictures. One close-up headshot and one full body. This will allow people who view your profile to know you are honest. Extra points if you can upload a photo with a group of friends. Most people show more interest if you look like you have friends. Have a photo of yourself taken in which you're doing some sort of activity. Many people, in shape or not, want someone

who looks like they get out of the house (even people who would rather stay home).

4. Learn the art of small talk. Using icebreakers and small talk is the best way to begin to connect. Be strategic with your questions. You can ask great, fun questions that don't intimidate but get you to understand the person more. Some apps support this by giving you prompts; some do not. Small talk is an art, and many people don't know what to do with that canvas.

5. Treat others the way you want to be treated. Don't lead people on. Don't engage if you just want to talk to someone to kill time until someone better comes along. Be kind, be polite, and be honest.

Conclusion

When I completed the fifth draft of this book, I was writing it one year and five months from the start of the healing related to my divorce. I just celebrated my 43rd birthday. I was speaking with one of my besties—the one who always sends me a birthday card in the mail (something to always look forward to). "Can you believe where I am at?" I asked, in shock. "You did this, you earned this, you did the things," she responded. We both reflected on how a year before, life had been painful not just for me, but for her, and she was the one consistent witness privileged to my journey of working through the pain.

A year before, I struggled through my birthday because I was still broken and fighting to put the pieces together. The week of my more recent birthday, I had started a new job I had fought to find. I had forgotten that my birthday was quickly approaching. I was training in my new job and received a call at the end of the week from my boss. She was working from home that day. She called to say happy birthday and I said thank you. I am a delayed processor by nature. I aim to delay my responses to ensure that my feelings are aligned with the situation. By the time I got off the phone with her, I felt a familiar emotion—one never welcomed, and not welcomed in

public. I was in a room of people who were all training for our jobs at this awesome organization. As I received floods of happy birthday wishes from those in the room, I couldn't breathe. I was diving rapidly into a panic attack and had to run out of the room. It was embarrassing. I had to find a corner in which to pull myself together. I was lucky because I was given an office at this company, so I ran into it and shut the door. I was in the dark, trying to catch my breath. I hadn't at that point, worked on my birthday in over 20 years. I was militant about that. I am a dedicated, loyal, hard worker who usually is nudged to take a vacation. But I would always proactively book that day off. I was in sheer panic because it was something I had forgotten in the chaos. I had forgotten me. However, I understood that I had a focus. Employment to afford my mortgage so I could keep my home for the kids. This was my number one priority, and I wasn't thinking of anything else. Including me. Once I calmed down, I realized that this one blunder was small compared to the reward I was receiving which was equitable work, and another day I kept my home. Sacrifices, whether we are aware of them or not, will occur during our healing. We must find our way back to the surface again, and sometimes this step can be missed. The following year, I took six days off to compensate. My boss was pleased with that decision.

You are here and that is great, especially if you have completed all the exercises. I will not lie to you—you are not exempt from bad days. But you now have many coping mechanisms to navigate those days and that is the point. I remember having a couple of bad weeks almost a year and a half after my divorce. I was crying and staring out my window questioning everything; however, I was reminded how far I had come with all the work I have done. I wish like hell that by the time you are reading these pages, a new, gorgeous, mindful, loving, careful significant other is in your life. God knows the positive energy you should have by now should attract that person. But here is the deal. I would like you to remember the following when you are feeling down:

1. Remember you journaled and captured some heavy stuff.
2. You purged your pain in prayer, journaling, conversation, therapy, and exercise.
3. You got active and off your couch even if you barely had the strength to lift a fork.
4. You dove into a hobby that you wanted to try. While you may or may not still be doing that hobby, you tried it. That is what matters.

This is a journey. Life is a journey. I ask you to forgive quickly, heal quicker, and move forward at lightning speed. There is no dress rehearsal. We do not get a second chance. We have one life. Live it. Love again. Enjoy the journey.

About the Author

Carli Lance has an unofficial PhD in heartbreak and breakups. Her education in love and loss started as a young child. Tumultuous relationships with family and friends, and her propensity to fall in love fast, led to several significant breakups as an adult including a divorce from a 10-year marriage that she didn't see coming.

However, Carli found a way to transform all that pain and channelled her incredible life experiences into a successful career as a writer, mentor, and coach. In Moving Forward: A Woman's Guide to Healing and Moving on After a Breakup, Carli shares her valuable insight and tips for how to empower yourself after you've had your heart broken so that you can heal faster and move forward to become the best possible version of you.

Carli is also passionate about wellness and is a devoted mother to her two amazing young sons.

Manufactured by Amazon.ca
Bolton, ON